W9-DHK-234

CROWNING PEAK OF NEW ZEALAND, MOUNT COOK SOARS TO 12,349 FEET.

SURPRISING LANDS DOWN UNDER

By Mary Ann Harrell

**Prepared by the Special Publications Division
National Geographic Society, Washington, D.C.**

SURPRISING LANDS DOWN UNDER

By MARY ANN HARRELL

Published by THE NATIONAL GEOGRAPHIC
  SOCIETY
GILBERT M. GROSVENOR
  President and Chairman of the Board
MELVIN M. PAYNE, THOMAS W. MCKNEW,
  Chairmen Emeritus
OWEN R. ANDERSON, *Executive Vice President*
ROBERT L. BREEDEN, *Senior Vice President,*
  Publications and Educational Media

Prepared by The Special Publications Division
DONALD J. CRUMP, *Director*
PHILIP B. SILCOTT, *Associate Director*
BONNIE S. LAWRENCE, *Assistant Director*

Staff for this Book
SEYMOUR L. FISHBEIN, *Managing Editor*
THOMAS B. POWELL III, *Illustrations Editor*
VIVIANE Y. SILVERMAN, *Art Director*
DEBRA A. ANTONINI, LORI ELIZABETH DAVIE,
  ANN NOTTINGHAM KELSALL,
  BARBARA A. PAYNE, *Researchers*

RICHARD M. CRUM, TONI EUGENE,
  MARY ANN HARRELL, JANE R. MCCAULEY,
  H. ROBERT MORRISON, *Picture Legend Writers*
JOHN D. GARST, JR., SUSAN I. FRIEDMAN,
  GARY M. JOHNSON, *Map Research*
  and Production
TIBOR G. TOTH, *Map Relief*
MICKI MORAN, *Computer Map Lab*
SANDRA F. LOTTERMAN, *Editorial Assistant*
ARTEMIS S. LAMPATHAKIS,
  Illustrations Assistant

Engraving, Printing, and Product Manufacture
GEORGE V. WHITE, *Director,* and
  VINCE P. RYAN, *Manager, Manufacturing and*
  Quality Management
DAVID V. SHOWERS, *Production Manager*
KEVIN HEUBUSCH, *Production*
  Project Manager

Lewis R. Bassford, *Assistant
  Production Manager*
Kathleen M. Cirucci, Timothy H. Ewing,
  Senior Production Assistants
Carol Curtis, *Senior Production Staff Assistant*
Susan A. Bender, Catherine G. Cruz,
  Marisa J. Farabelli, Karen Katz,
  Lisa A. LaFuria, Eliza Morton,
  Dru Stancampiano, Marilyn J. Williams,
  Staff Assistants
Elisabeth MacRae-Bobynskyj, *Indexer*

*Tongariro National Park in
New Zealand grew out of a
Maori chieftain's gift, to
preserve volcanic heights held
sacred in ancestral lore.*

TERRY HANN/COMMUNICATE NZ

Contents

*On burnished sands of earth's most
arid inhabited continent an Aborigine
holds spear tips and a killing stick,
symbolizing the saga of adaptation
and survival by Australia's first people
across some 10 millennia.*

ROBIN SMITH / ODYSSEY / STONE WORLDWIDE

Prologue:
Two Flags in the South

"It's so remote here, so far away from its neighbors . . . beyond hundreds of miles of seas, often wild and desperate seas," mused Peter McLeavey, owner of a Wellington art gallery. "We must be the most isolated nation in the world." Peter is a fourth-generation New Zealander, and like people I met all over the country, he was giving a good deal of thought to his nation's identity and fortunes as its 150th anniversary approached—1990 is its sesquicentennial year. Like them, he emphasized its lonely position in the southwest Pacific. And like them, I expect, he would be politely exasperated with anyone who confused New Zealand with Australia.

I never met one, but I've heard of tourists who thought Sydney's famous Harbour Bridge links Australia and New Zealand, and wanted to know how long it would take to drive across. In fact the quickest jetliners take three hours. I can see how people halfway round the world confuse the two countries—they're English-speaking nations, former colonies, now prominent in the Commonwealth of Nations that has succeeded the British Empire.

They're countries that Americans dream of visiting: "I've *always*

Master mariner James Cook braved the waves Britannia would rule. He explored New Zealand and Australia's east coast, staking claims for Britain. An Aboriginal artist painted a sailing ship on rock in northern Australia (above).

Though Cook tore the veils from Terra Australis Incognita *and placed Australia and New Zealand in true relation, many in the Western world still deem them near neighbors. At their closest, these English-speaking nations of the South Seas lie 927 miles apart.*

MAP DESIGN BY SUSIE I. FRIEDMAN

wanted to go there." They're full of friendly, easygoing people who welcome—and argue with—visiting Yanks. Yet they're as different as kindred nations can be, and they like it that way.

I had visited both, all too briefly, in the past and wanted to go back. Now I looked forward to exploring both. I would go from the subtropical mildness of New Zealand's North Island to the thick-wool-and-hot-porridge chill of its southern counterpart; from the enormous central emptiness of Australia to its enormous cities. I would learn the varied traditions of four peoples: the voyagers who reached New Zealand a thousand years ago, and those who came within two centuries; the explorers whose past in Australia may exceed 40,000 years, and those who came as recently as a year ago.

When the six colonies of Australia were warily planning to form a single federal government, just before the turn of the century, they invited New Zealand to join in. A classic explanation of New Zealanders' reaction came from the statesman Sir Joseph Ward: "There're 1,201 reasons why we won't join Australia. Twelve hundred of them are miles. The one is that we don't want to."

Thus, as a New Zealand commission reported at the time, the southern seas would hold "two British Powers instead of one." Both nations adopted the British blue ensign as their flag, with the Union Jack in the upper left and the Southern Cross as a badge. Significantly, some Australians would prefer a completely different design to express a new and different identity, and the bicentennial year of 1988—the 200th anniversary of the arrival of the First Fleet colonists from England—inspired them to speak up. If anyone was redesigning the New Zealand flag, I didn't hear of it.

Historic links began with the first great voyage of Britain's masterly explorer James Cook. From October 1769, through the following March, he mapped New Zealand's shores. Then he sailed westward and, after 19 days at sea, he sighted the southeast corner of Australia, naming his landfall Point Hicks, and worked his way northward.

Cook described the New Zealand natives as "a brave open warlike people," thought the Australian natives "a timorous and inoffensive race." He claimed territory in New Zealand and eastern Australia for George III. Dutch navigators had discovered "Nova Zeelandia" and the western coast of Australia, calling the land "Nova Hollandia," more than a century earlier, but the Dutch had pressed no claims. A TV miniseries made Cook a family hero for the bicentennial. On a fine summer afternoon in December, I boarded a paddle steamer on Australia's Murray River—"our little brown rope of a river," a friend said fondly—for an excursion. As skipper Max Carrington came down the riverbank with his white cap, a little blond girl hailed him: "The captain's coming, Captain Cook!"

British ties, southern skies: New Zealand's flag has four stars in the Southern Cross. Australia uses five, and a large seven-pointed one for its six states and territories.

Australians describe their homeland as the world's largest island and smallest continent, oldest, flattest, and driest. (Antarctica gets less precipitation, but who runs sheep or cattle there?) Professor Eric Willmot has called it the "ugliest place on earth," a land of "secret beauty" that only those possessed by her can know. Much of the terrain is vermilion, an astonishing orange red, and none of it gave white settlers an easy time; it often gets credit for their notorious profanity. In area it matches the 48 contiguous states of the United States if you subtract Illinois, and in its bicentennial year it supported about 16 million people.

New Zealand's home islands, with about 3.4 million residents, roughly equal the area of Colorado. The North Island is a bit smaller than Pennsylvania, the South a bit smaller than Florida, Stewart Island about half the size of Little Rhody. Rolling hills, snowcapped peaks, and dramatic shores seem designed for travel posters and rich grazing. Frequent earthquakes inspired the nickname the "Shaky Isles," which appeals especially to Australian sportswriters.

The Kiwis—the people take this nickname from the flightless bird of the islands—and the Aussies swap taunts like rival brothers, but they're allies against the rest of the world and they have ideals in common. One is mateship, the bond between men who face adversity together—floods or bushfires, bosses, enemies in arms. Another is egalitarianism. Nothing but competence should justify superior rank, and that rank shouldn't need a lot of deference. These are themes of the great binational myth known as the Anzac legend.

The southern dominions pledged full support to Britain when she fought Germany and the Ottoman Empire in World War I. Young men volunteered—to find adventure, to serve the empire, to prove that colonials were worthy of the mother country. There was, a historian noted, "a haze of rather splendid feeling."

Anzac—from Australian and New Zealand Army Corps—designates not only the men but also a place, a cove on the Turkish coast. The British command meant to wrest the vital Dardanelles strait from the Turks. At dawn on April 25, 1915, the colonials were put ashore: on the wrong beach, under Turkish fire from the cliffs above. New Zealand novelist Maurice Shadbolt calls it a campaign "planned by posturing louts and orchestrated by elegant lunatics."

Amateurs learning fast, the Anzacs fought their way inland, up barren ridges in a haze of lead. They hacked trenches into rocky dust until "digger" became a synonym for soldier. They took, and inflicted, staggering losses. The homelands thrilled with pride as reports of their sons' valor at Gallipoli outran the news of casualties.

By August the Anzacs, wasted by illness and exhaustion and frustrated by the incompetence of higher command, lost even the dimmest hope of victory. In heat like the outback's, the Anzac uniform was boots and shorts, sunburn and lice. A blizzard, deadly as a storm in New Zealand's mountains, struck in November; sentries froze to death on their feet, rifle in hand. In January 1916 the survivors were evacuated, to fight in France.

April 25, Anzac Day, is a unique day in Australia and New Zealand, a day of coming of age for both nations. Veterans—of later wars, now—march in procession, and lay wreaths at memorial shrines. On Anzac Day in Auckland, a grandmother showed me pictures of a small grandson and his big sister: "We bake burned cookies together," she remarked with a smile. Then she told me how pleased she was that young people were taking part in the observance—"to know why they're free, with schools to go to, and food on the table: because of the men who went overseas and fought."   ◼

April 25, Anzac Day, at the Shrine of Remembrance in Melbourne. The guard's World War I uniform honors the Australian and New Zealand Army Corps—the Anzacs, whose bravery bonded the two nations in pride.

INDIAN OCEAN
JAVA SEA
CORAL SEA
PACIFIC
1939 - 45
WAS DEDICATED
BY
HER MAJESTY
QUEEN ELIZABETH II
25TH FEBRUARY 1954

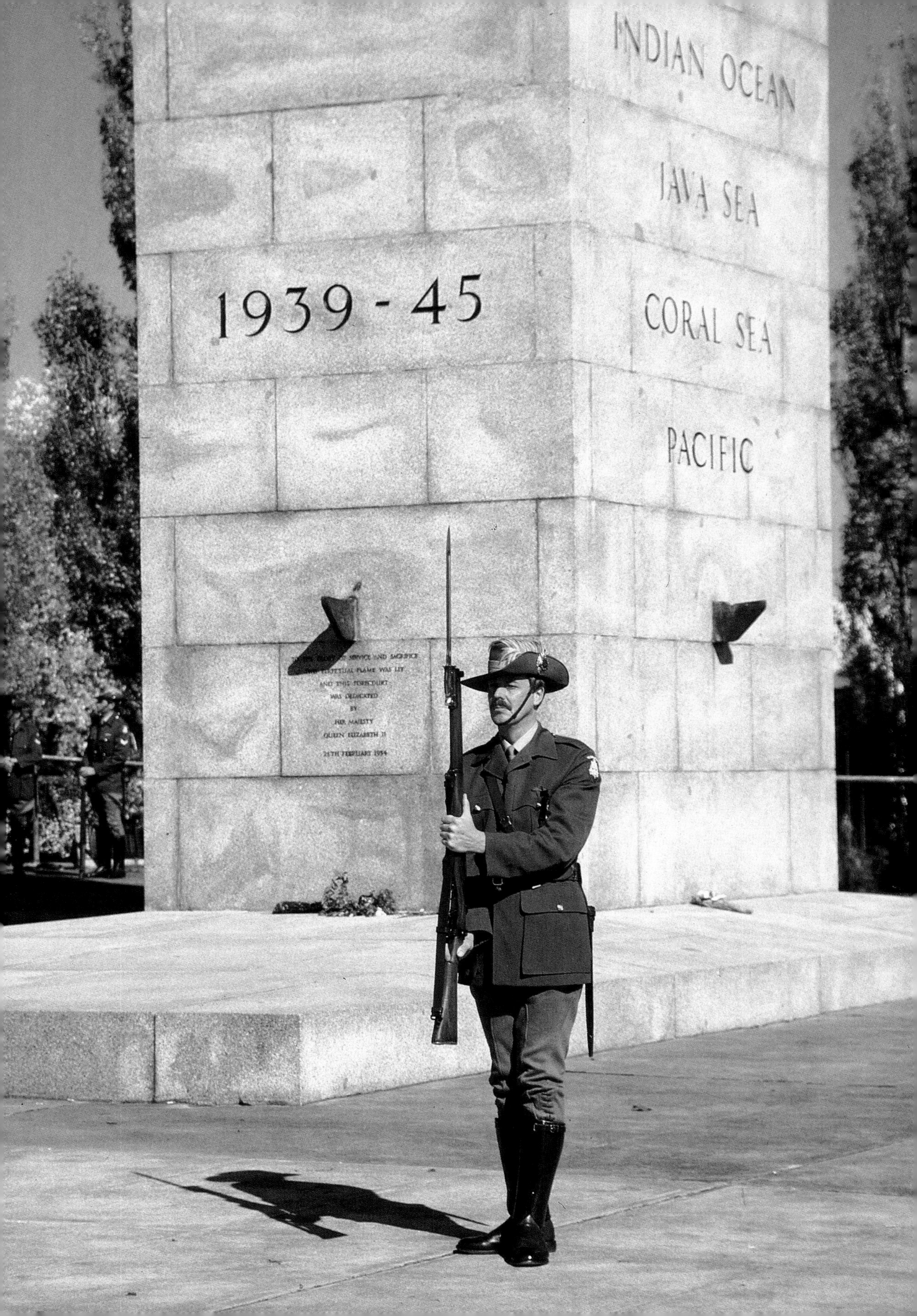

NEW

JULY SKIERS REST IN THE REMARKABLES ABOVE LAKE WAKATIPU AND QUEENSTOWN

Under the Long, Long Winds

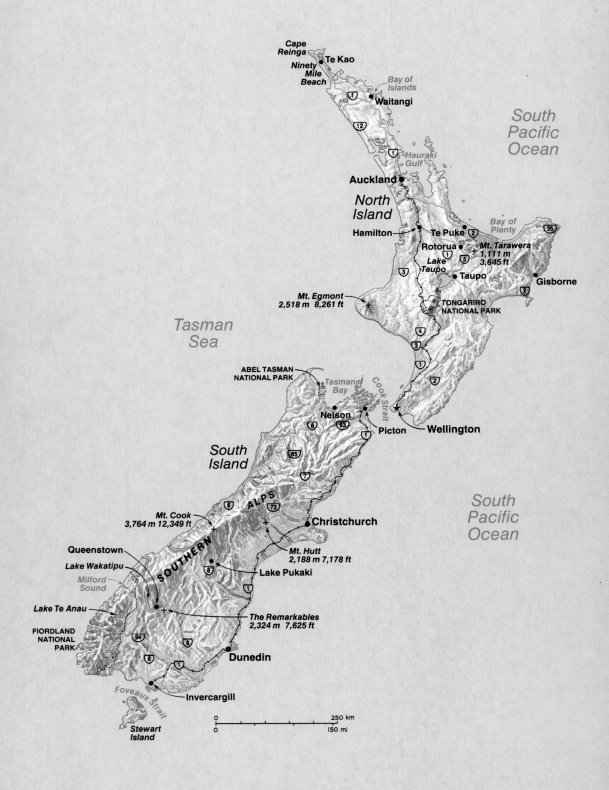

Isles of High Mountains

From southern rivers of ice and fjord-cut cliffs to a balmy taper in the north, the islands stretch across a thousand miles. Between fjords and sunny beaches lie tranquil pastures, steaming geysers and volcanic cones, modern cities and Maori shrines—no place more than 80 miles from the sea. Steep terrain gives the land awesome, uncluttered vistas. "Let me tell you about my country," writes a poet, "how it dreams in small towns." To Polynesian seafarers, ancestors of the Maori, the islands appeared as Aotearoa—The Land of the Long White Cloud. Scholars suggest the first voyagers arrived about a thousand years ago, making this land one of the last to be inhabited by humans. British and Maori figures in the coat of arms (above) acknowledge the nation's bicultural traditions.

The North Island:
Seascapes and Geysers

Another rainbow curved over the Auckland hills, shimmering above the suburban houses on their quarter-acre lots. Showers and sunlight had spattered us on a winter Sunday outing, a family excursion with the Craddocks: Sue and businessman Owen and the children. Our route had zigzagged through the isthmus on which New Zealand's largest city spreads, the land pinched between waters of the South Pacific and the Tasman Sea.

We had admired the metropolis from the summit of Mount Eden, matching built-up areas to the empty vistas in a grandparent's snapshots. We had splashed through puddles to the War Memorial Museum, with its notable collection of Maori wood carving and relics of combat ranging from a long Maori canoe to World War II aircraft. Rainbows had appeared at intervals, and I said something about how lovely they are. "Yeah," said Michael Craddock, a laconic blond teenager. "We're trying to find a way to export them."

Overseas trade has been gaining importance in New Zealand ever since the white men's ships began hanging around in the 1790s. Today the country's comfortable life-style depends on it, as Michael's joke acknowledged; export problems had *(Continued on page 26)*

Maori art transforms a house post into an image of ancestral homage. Flashing eyes signify a living presence; protruding tongue flaunts defiance.

NATIONAL MUSEUM OF NEW ZEALAND: TE WHARE TAONGA O AOTEAROA / TERRY HANN-COMMUNICATE NZ

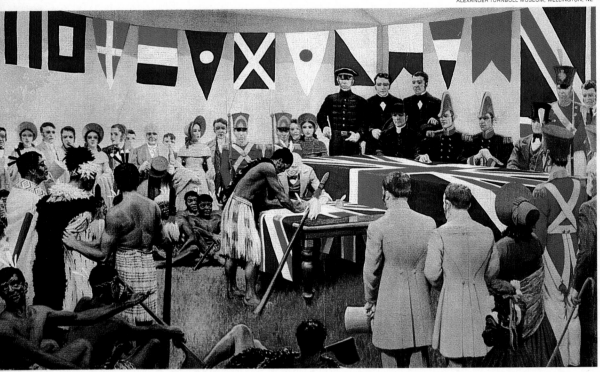

Accepting Britain's sovereign as their own, Maori chiefs sign the Treaty of Waitangi—an artist's version of New Zealand's founding in 1840. Today many Maori honor a queen of their own, Te Arikinui Dame Te Atairangikaahu (right) or, informally, Dame Te Ata. On formal occasions the Queen dons a kiwi-feather cloak, worn here with a whalebone pendant. Jade pendants in stylized human form, like that at left, imply high rank; called heitiki, *they often descend as heirlooms. In her hair the Queen wears feathers of the extinct huia bird, symbol of ultimate rank.*

*Elaborate carvings depict notable ancestors and tribal
histories at the Whare Runanga—Meetinghouse—in Waitangi,
where the British and Maori signed their treaty. Grasping
a club, a Maori performer with eyes bulging and tongue thrust
out demonstrates a traditional gesture to frighten an enemy.
Face painting recalls the custom of tattooing—a warrior's
reward for bravery in battle and a badge of chieftainship.*

WINTON CLEAL / COMMUNICATE NZ (ABOVE AND UPPER RIGHT);
YVA MOMATIUK / JOHN EASTCOTT (RIGHT)

JOHN KING / PHOTOBANK IMAGE LIBRARY-NEW ZEALAND; WARREN JACOBS (RIGHT)

*Ablaze with December bloom, the pohutukawa
tree ornaments the coasts at Christmastime.
Instead of snow and sleigh bells, North Islanders
associate the Yuletide with hot sunshine and
the pohutukawa in its glory. Shipwrights of
yesteryear shaped the durable timber into keels.
Above the surf a lone pohutukawa (opposite)
defies the headland winds on Cape Reinga—The
Leaping Place of the Spirits. Here, according
to Maori legend, came the spirits of the dead, to a
gnarled old tree, down a withered root, leaping
into the depths for the journey to the otherworld.*

turned into a crisis for farmers. But if you can't export rainbows and glaciers, or trout streams and ski slopes, you can welcome visitors; and more than half a million people a year come to enjoy a holiday. If they arrive on the North Island, it's probably at Auckland. Here I began a journey through proud cities and green farmlands where top-soil is measured in feet, to snow-crowned ranges and steaming gey-sers, onto headlands where wild seas collide and Maori legend lives.

Auckland shows urban life at its most lavish. With two spacious harbors winding in from east and west, it's the "city of sails" in a na-tion of good sailors—and good sailmakers, adds Ken Larsen. Ken, a rugby enthusiast who teaches literature at the University of Auck-land, showed me some of his favorite spots.

"You have family beaches on the east coast—white sand, mild waves: the sort of thing we all grow up with. The west coast beaches are far more rugged, fierce; they remind one of that California stretch at Big Sur." The sand is black, from its iron content. "The Japanese pick it up and mix it with seawater to make sludge and take it back to Japan to make steel." At Piha we crossed the black beach for a view of Lion Rock, which does resemble the lion of em-pire gazing moodily out to sea. "There's great surfing here."

In the Waitakere hills Ken eased his car up steep lanes. Kauri trees and sweeping tree ferns caught my eye; this is a reserve of na-tive forest, a remnant of the bush. "There's a certain blackness in the air," said Ken. "The dark greens soak up the light. Australian light is far more vibrant; deserts make it that way."

Sundown colors rippled on the western harbor as we drove to the Larsen home. Apricot trees flourish beside the house, sheltered by a ridge from the cold southerlies and facing north for sunlight and warm winds. I came to expect that in the Southern Hemisphere, and yet it never seemed natural. The house looks out on the low cone of Rangitoto Island, a shield volcano in Waitemata Harbour, inactive for more than 250 years. Harbor views had convinced Ken to make his career in Auckland.

"Auckland's the jam on the bread in a trans-Tasman tour," says Dame Catherine Tizard, the mayor, a chic white-haired woman of in-tense energy. When I met her, she was concerned—among many other issues—with the new Aotea Centre, a performing-arts complex rising in the heart of town. "The Centre will be a national symbol. We'll attract people who wouldn't come all this way just to see a few beauty spots and a few sheep; and a lamb chop eaten here can pro-vide six jobs more than a lamb chop shipped abroad. Besides, we've lacked a venue for major artistic events." This in a metropolis that holds more than a fourth of New Zealand's population.

That's about 900,000 people, and 2 in 10 are Polynesian. The lat-ter include nearly 100,000 Maori, *tangata whenua* or people of the land, descendants of the first settlers. There are also some 82,000 Pa-cific islanders for whom New Zealand is the big nation, the bright lights, the place of opportunity. Dame Cath can extend greetings in five Polynesian languages. At times she must deal with delicate complications. In Maori custom, political rituals and realities are matters for men; they must keep it so or lose *mana*, which means prestige, power, authority with divine sanction. "But as mayor," said Dame Cath, "I must uphold the mana of my office."

Her election, in 1983, underlined a change in the attitudes of white New Zealanders, who also had strong convictions about the roles of women. When she campaigned in 1980, a military parade took place just before the election. The incumbent mayor, a man, took the salute. "There you have it," pronounced a male spectator; "you need a man in office. A woman couldn't do that properly." A lady nearby spoke up, gently: "I'm sure you're quite right—but don't you think someone should inform the Queen?"

Fixed notions of a woman's place and the gentle, tweaking response—both are part of the old New Zealand, according to a brisk young lawyer named Patrick Driscoll. "*Which* New Zealand do you want to see?" he asked. "There's no consensus any more, not even about football! We used to be two small islands just off the southwest coast of Britain, with a narrow band of experience, a lot of conformity. That's not true any longer."

Anne Culpan, Dame Cath's daughter, made a similar point about her generation. "After uni [university] we went abroad in boatloads for the big O.E. You weren't credible as a young professional without Overseas Experience." I had heard of second- and third-generation New Zealanders who referred to Britain as home. "I loved it in the U.K.," said Anne, "but I didn't feel it was my home."

Frontier habits and values have marked life in Godzone—God's Own Country, a nickname that has acquired a note of self-mockery. "The pioneering ethic's still rampant here," Campbell Hegan told me. He's one of the potters who started after World War II and have made New Zealand ceramics famous. "No technology—we had to live in the country, dig our own clay, cut our own wood," Campbell recalled. "We built enormous kilns with bricks we humped up the hill." He spent ten years on his distinctive sang de boeuf glaze, an oxblood red. When I met him he was firing his ware in a state-of-the-art kiln in his Devonport studio: "space technology—hasn't even got bricks. That's dinner-jacket firing."

Even as they welcome technology, New Zealanders cling to frontier ways. Don't hire it, do-it-yourself—remains the homeowner's norm. I found Anne and Dave Harkness renovating a villa in Mount Eden, an old suburb being gentrified. Anne, a radiologist who plays field hockey, and Dave, engineer and triathlete, had hung blue-and-white wallpaper in the dining room and were redoing the kitchen. The work in progress had little effect on the cuisine—a suave duck-and-brandy pâté and lamb steaks in a subtle kiwifruit marinade.

It seemed worlds away from that old Down Under standby, spaghetti on toast, and even further from the kind of barbed teasing that frequently spices life in the islands. I recall one recipe for a prank on departing honeymooners that made me wince for the victims: "You hide a bit of fish in the car's hubcaps. It gets pretty ripe, and they have a time finding it."

In another part of Auckland I saw what my guides called the "lowest end of the scale." Otara had been planned as a model suburb. It was now a Polynesian area and looked well kept and attractive to me. But there were tensions between the island groups. "There's a fair bit of ill-feeling here," I was told in good Kiwi understatement.

The churches strive to reconcile these groups. So does the Youth Resource Centre in Auckland. Rendy Faaloua, a poised girl from Western Samoa, showed me about and introduced me to Wana Nopera, the manager. Wana explained the ground rules—no alcohol, no drugs—and the programs: leadership courses in legal rights, training in vocational skills and multicultural understanding. "If we do ourselves out of a job, we've done what we set out to do," she said.

I watched dancers rehearsing in a room that serves as a *marae* (literally, a "courtyard"; the Maori place of assembly). Young women performed a dance of welcome, their hands fluttering like wind-tossed leaves. Young men stamped the floor and slapped their thighs in a *haka*, a dance of challenge that once stirred warriors to battle.

Dances and songs like these have entertained visitors for years. Today the arts of Maori culture express a new pride, a new defiance. White reaction varies. Officials like Dame Cath and institutions like the University of Auckland seek to honor the Maori heritage in their ceremonies. But I also encountered the attitude that people Down Under call redneck. One young man waved a magazine article at me, ridiculing its praise of Maori society: "Biggest load of codswallop I ever read! This 'wonderful South Pacific society'—it was based on slavery and cannibalism and tribal wars and genocide!"

In 1990 New Zealand has a 150th anniversary, which few in 1988 seemed eager to discuss. "It's a matter of great sensitivity at the moment," said Dame Cath. The event to be celebrated took place on what is today the Waitangi National Reserve, a gem of the northeast coast on the Bay of Islands, about four hours from Auckland by road. I saw more spectacular settings in New Zealand, but nothing lovelier. White mist hid the crests of dark islands on a rainy winter morning; a bellbird's song rang like wind chimes on the mild air.

Here on February 6, 1840, a British official and Maori chiefs signed the Treaty of Waitangi. Its three short articles extended the protection of Queen Victoria to the Maori, gave them the rights of British subjects, confirmed their possession of their property, and took in return the chiefs' gift of—what? "Sovereignty," in the English text; *kawanatanga*, or governance, in the Maori version. The tribes had no experience of European sovereigns.

With a Maori friend I inspected the Residency, or "Treaty

House," a handsome frame building, and the *Whare Runanga*, the Maori meetinghouse built for the centenary in 1940. Its lavish carvings follow many tribal styles, to represent all Maori people; its woven reed panels, of step fret and diamond designs, show pan-Maori patterns; on the rafters white scroll designs carry the motif of a fern frond unfolding. Plaques honor the two peoples, *nga iwi e rua*, Maori and Pakeha. Maori, by the way, means "normal" or "usual." Nobody knows the meaning of Pakeha, the designation for whites.

New Zealanders have taken pride in their country's honorable beginning as a partnership of equals. In 1840 the Maori were the more numerous and the stronger. They had welcomed the Pakeha—traders from Australia, whalers and sealers from New England, missionaries from England and Scotland—who brought new food crops, iron nails, and firearms. Guns altered the scope of tribal wars. "All this country is strewn with the blood and bones of my ancestors," says Maori leader Matiu Rata in the far north. Guns also held the white settlers in check.

When the Maori felt themselves wronged, by threats to their mana or to tribal lands, they took up arms against the British. Warfare on the North Island lasted from 1845 to 1872. In an early engagement British field artillery bombarded a *pa*, or fortified site, for a week. "This," noted a major, "will astonish the weak minds of the natives." The natives, however, had devised a shellproof system of dugouts and bunkers. They came aboveground only to destroy a British storming party.

"It's a myth that the British here had incompetent officers," historian James Belich told me. "It took a major war to get the really lousy British generals out of their clubrooms and into the field. The real reason the British had difficulty is that the Maori were intelligent and disciplined, as well as brave and chivalrous. But they didn't have an empire to supply them; their warriors had to go home to grow their crops." In the end the Maori lost millions of acres of land.

Since 1975 a special Waitangi Tribunal has been working to redress old wrongs. Its findings bring hope to many Maori and disquiet to some Pakeha. I heard uneasy talk of actual conflict. Mat Rata scoffs at that: "How do you declare war on your brother-in-law?"

Mixed, or "bicultural," marriages aren't uncommon here, and I encountered a delightful example at Te Puke, a town of 5,000, "Kiwifruit Capital of the World." Brigid and Milton Peters—she's Anglo-Irish, he's Maori—had 15 acres of prime land, a foot of topsoil over freely draining pumice. When I went out to see the kiwi vines, their fruit had already been picked. "You do hard pruning in winter," said Milton, describing the seasons' round. "The vines fruit on first-year wood. They flower in the spring—September, October—and we bring the bees in, about 55 hives for 15 acres. At harvest a good gang will pick a hundred 12-bushel bins a day." Milton stopped to chat with a neighbor, Craig Scowan, a self-styled "authentic Kiwi—into beer, racing, and rugby, with beer being the best of the three." As the small talk and joking went on, Milton pointed to a robust green weed by my right foot. "That's *puha*—Maori spinach," he grinned. "Good with roast Pakeha."

At a local packing plant we watched the brown fruit jiggling along a conveyor belt—a Disney cartoon sequence loose in real life— while the graders sorted it. They kept only the best, counting 46 of the smallest to a tray, 25 of the largest, all prime quality ready for cold storage and shipment. And the export problem.

"We've never had to worry about the world market before," Brigid told me after dinner, "but other countries are growing kiwifruit now. And our dollar's high on world exchanges. That's hard on exporters. We may have to sell the orchard. Our neighbors offer to help. Trouble . . . that's when you know the goodness of people."

Near Gisborne topsoil that looks like fudge lies 17 to 20 feet deep on the river flats. The international date line lies just to the east, making Gisborne one of the first cities in the world to greet a new day. Here rise the white cliffs known as Young Nicks Head, named by Captain Cook in honor of Nicholas Young, the cabin boy who made the first sighting of land in October 1769.

July snow whitened the ridgetops, but the lowlands were frost free—spread with citrus orchards, vineyards, fields of broccoli and capsicum. "You'd say green peppers," observed my host Ross Shaw, an airline pilot home on leave. A few months earlier Cyclone Bola had dumped 36 inches of rain in the region. "See the vineyards?" asked Ross. "Bola flooded all that property. School kids came and dug the silt from around the roots to save the vines."

"It's our hills," said Ernie Langford, Ross's father-in-law. "The water runs off them so fast. The erosion's shocking. Our river's had more silt than the Yellow River in China."

"Farmers stripped all the native bush," explained Ross, "and the land started slipping." We stopped at a small, unheralded reserve called Gray's Bush in honor of a pioneer who had spared a bit of forest. It was magical: tall kahikatea, so-called white pine, reaching up into sunlight, nikau palms crowded in shadow. "The flats would have been smothered in this bush when Cook arrived," said Ross.

"This very earth speaks Maori," Mere Clarke told me. She and her husband, Miki, interpret the earth and its life for visitors. Mere and I drove out to Rongopai, a Maori meetinghouse dating from 1888, famed for its colorful paintings; here rich scrollwork offsets portraits in Pakeha folk-art style. En route Mere didn't linger in flood-damaged areas. "There's nothing worse than coming out to see people's plights," she said. Once she slowed at a fine orange orchard, branches sagging with small globes golden in the sun. "There're so many people starving in the world—how do we get our lovely fruit out to their countries?"

With one casual remark, Mere summed up the delight of New Zealand: "Everyone has beautiful scenery."

There's a youthful beauty in the unfinished terrain of the volcanic belt. Near Rotorua the Waimangu Valley holds one of the newest geothermal areas in the world. It appeared after Mount Tarawera blew apart in June 1886, and, unlike other parts of New Zealand's thermal region, Waimangu's youthful beauty remains unspoiled.

I toured it one day in the company of geologist Brad Scott and Averill Adlam of the District Council, who calls herself a conservationist "although that tends to be a dirty word." Brad talked proudly of the valley: "New Zealand's only undisturbed thermal area—no dams, no boreholes—and one of the best documented."

He said some North Island volcanoes, like the beautiful Ruapehu and Egmont, eject andesite in moderate amounts. These erupt frequently. In contrast, every few thousand years the rhyolite volcanoes explode and spew 300 or 400 cubic kilometers of molten material. "When these big volcanoes become restless," he concluded in a choice flourish of Kiwi style, "they manifest themselves very well."

Nobody left the path as we hiked down the valley. I saw bare soil, warm enough to kill vegetation, in Southern Crater. This ground, I thought, is *alive*. Farther on, in one jade green pool, patches of hot bubbles swirled over a hidden vent. A clear *cheep cheep cheep* alerted us to a fantail perched on a shrub, its tail feathers spread astern. Nearby, a lakeside geyserlet plashed up white in the sun every few minutes, only to subside into foam. Lovely. But as a local map note says, there's "an atmosphere of quiescent unearthly violence." With minimal warning an eruption in 1917 reamed out Frying Pan Flat and flipped the roof off a hilltop hotel.

I had visited Rotorua in the 1970s and looked forward to seeing it again. I recalled its zany mix of attractions: geysers, Maori artists, white-clad Pakeha playing lawn bowls among clumps of scarlet cannas and discreet signs warning "Beware of poison gas." Hydrogen sulfide charges the air here. Its rotten-egg pungency didn't deter the tourists who came for generations to the "Gateway to Geyserland." But the geysers are disappearing.

"Before 1950 New Zealand had about 130 geysers," said Averill Adlam; "now there're fewer than 10. In the '50s the government decided to generate electricity at Wairakei. Vast quantities of geothermal heat have been drawn off there, and we've lost 30 geysers at Wairakei and 3 at Lake Taupo. They dammed the Waikato River in the '60s and we lost 90." Rotoruans drilled private boreholes for swimming pools and spas, some 800 wells by the '80s, and, Averill added, the town's geysers "started to stop." A fight has been going on, with conservationists keen to ban access to the thermal field and a Users' Association determined to keep it.

· "We shouldn't have to go to Yellowstone Park to see a geyser!" Averill declared, as we went out to Whakarewarewa, the thermal area in a Maori community. We waited to see if Pohutu, grandest of them all, would perform. Pohutu muttered and rumbled and sent a giant white plume roaring up into white and chilly mist.

Businessman Trevor Prichard of the Users' Association lives in a spacious split-level, in a zone where the private bores have been sealed. The users, he said, are not "affluent greedies"—many are retired persons. He told me about a neighbor who couldn't use his spa any longer to ease severe arthritis. This man, he said, had been told by a cabinet minister, "You've had it too good for too long."

Without doubt, New Zealand has had it good. In the 1950s, former Prime Minister David Lange has written, New Zealand was one of the five wealthiest countries in the world: "Today we rank twenty-fifth." His government undertook to end an era of subsidies and protection for the economy, to let market realities have free play. Not too many years ago, I was told, the minister of labour would know the unemployed by name—all six of them. It was all 116,798 of them by June 1988: one out of every eleven in the work force. When it was just 92,788 the previous year, one out of every three New Zealanders was getting cash benefits from the state.

"Is there anything, we ask, which the State cannot set right? And the reply to our query is, Nothing." So, in 1899, one colonist defined public expectations. Government should assure a fair go for everyone—a fair go, or fair chance, is a powerful ideal Down Under.

"It can be embarrassing to confront the old expectations," James Belich of Victoria University was saying one morning in his Wellington office. "In the Victorian era some foresaw a population of a hundred million here by A.D. 2000. We have a fascinating, tumultuous past, and a lot of Pakeha have no knowledge of it."

As he spoke a deep hum became audible. The room—on the top floor of a nine-story building—lifted and sidled like a canoe on the swash of a ship; the floor throbbed as if a huge engine had started up beneath us. We were having an earthquake. "A big one," remarked Dr. Belich calmly: 4.7 on the Richter scale, as it turned out. But not the Big One, luckily. A major fault system passes through Wellington, the capital city. Bush-crowned hills ring the harbor—which lies leaden or whitecapped or glittering as the weather varies with the winds of the Roaring Forties—and frame houses with magnificent views perch optimistically on unnerving slopes.

At the foot of one hill the avenue called The Terrace traces a fault line between glass-sheathed towers. Nearby are the neoclassical Parliament buildings and the contemporary cone known as the Beehive, where cabinet ministers have their offices. In form, the state is a monarchy, under Elizabeth II, Queen of New Zealand. In practice, democracy rules through the majority party in Parliament.

"Bills don't become law until I deliver what we call the Royal Assent." His Excellency the Governor-General explained his role when I had the honor of meeting him at his official residence, Government House. The Most Reverend Sir Paul Reeves, who was Anglican Archbishop of New Zealand before his civil appointment in 1985, blends calm dignity with the unstarched ease of an athlete. "I represent the Crown—the principles, really, that we seek to apply in government. We don't have a written constitution; we rely on a lot of precedent, and on trust." He is of Maori descent through his mother.

Two queens, not one, play a role in New Zealand. The resident is the Maori Queen, Te Arikinui Dame Te Atairangikaahu. Or, informally, Dame Te Ata. Sixth of her line, she inherited a dignity dating from 1858. By then, powerful chiefs had concluded that the British took strength from unity under one monarch and the Maori should have a king of their own. The King Movement sought to end tribal wars and secure tribal lands, to uphold the Maori's rights and their mana. Dame Te Ata succeeded her father in 1966, and in May her people gather at Turangawaewae Marae, near Hamilton, to celebrate the anniversary of her coronation. I was lucky enough to attend, with a former secretary of the Queen's, Ina Te Uira, as hostess, interpreter, and guide in etiquette.

"Nothing is more important than human relationships," Ina told me, "and the King Movement is an expression of cohesion, of Maori cohesion in spite of the pressures of Western society."

I also heard the King Movement described as a last desperate effort to stop the confiscation and sale of lands. If it failed in that, it has preserved pride and *aroha*, or love. "Not as when I see a beautiful woman," an elder explained; "this is not that love. As when you see many people and think, you're going to get a lot more friend."

Through a rainy, happy weekend I learned the rituals of welcome—vital in the times of warfare when guests or hosts might be plotting treachery, getting a lot more enemy. On formal occasions even today, as visitors arrive, always in groups, they pause outside the marae. The ranking elder intones a protective chant. An older woman of the host group stands before the meetinghouse and gives the *karanga*, a high-pitched wailing cry that calls the dead as well as the living. *Haere mai*—welcome—*haere mai!*

"Whenever I hear the karanga," my friend Brigid Peters had said, "I seem to see the land as it was in the beginning: the dark bush, and the mist on the hills."

Song and chant gave life to the past. Dancers in the cultural competitions wore the *piupiu*, or flax kilts of tradition. When I met chef Neha Tahapeehi, he was wearing a white toque and gulping a meat pie, a Down Under staple, and he laughed when I asked about the earth ovens of Polynesian antiquity. "We're feeding two or three thousand—we need push-button cooking!"

But to honor one dignitary—the first Roman Catholic bishop of

Maori stock—a barefoot kilted warrior dashed forward in ritual challenge; he laid a carved stick at the feet of the visitor. Bishop Takuira Mariu, in cassock and biretta, gravely picked up the baton as proof that he came in peace. Despite the language barrier, I enjoyed the eloquence of the orators, whose gestures have the force of a dancer's and whose phrasing suggests an aria. As a courtesy to Princess Abigail Kekaulike Kawananakoa of the Hawaiian royal family, an elder of the Ngati Porou tribe spoke in English: "I married a beautiful Pakeha girl, but she died." A pause. He spread his arms with a great smile: "Princess! I am free!" Royalty smiled. The rest guffawed.

Tukoroirangi Morgan, a young TV journalist, had come from Auckland. "My grandparents and great-grandparents have been subjects of the Maori kings," he told me. "I come home for peace of mind. This is where my strength is." When he left, an elder who had overheard us leaned toward me. I expected philosophy; I got teasing. "I think," said he, with a twinkle, "you're a bloody flirter!"

Usually, men speak on the marae; then women sing. As a graceful girl named Manawa Tini put it, "The men take care of the heavy side of things, quarrels and grudges. The women do the soothing— they're not the aggressive sex." A few tribes do allow highborn women to speak, and Whaia McClutchie asserted her privilege with great effect, a sturdy white-haired woman with a resonant contralto.

"I've been Queen for 20 years but I can't speak like Whaia," said Dame Te Ata tactfully. Her voice was gentle but clear, and she spoke from the porch of Mahinarangi, the great carved meetinghouse that holds portraits and relics of her forebears. Her remarks, of greeting and thanks, met approving murmurs of "lovely! *Kia ora!*"

I remember her as the unassuming lady to whom Ina presented me at dawn, after a ceremonial raising of her standard. I remember Ina's hospitality—"we meet four times, and it's no more friends—it's family!" And I remember the music of the Ratana band, sustained and majestic and composed, measured like the great swells that bore the ancient canoes across the sea under the long, long winds.

Kupe the legendary explorer discovered this land and survived the perils of its waters. So I heard the story in northernmost Northland, where mountains shrink to hills and the land runs narrow between the Tasman Sea and the Pacific. I visited both shores near Te Kao with Raewyn Everitt and Loui Harris, sisters-in-law, each tossing out bits of local lore as we traveled: "You get a lot of crayfish here on the rocks of the east coast, and children learn to swim on these beaches. . . . You have picnics in summer, at Christmas. Your sea eggs are fat—that's sea-urchin roe—and the tops of the pohutukawa trees are red."

On the Tasman coast, at a spot called The Bluff, we reached the famous Ninety Mile Beach (about 60 miles, in fact). Here we climbed gargantuan rocks and gathered mussels tangy with brine. Great combers lashed the rocks, and I remembered the victory chant that sings of "the swift-driving wave of the battle."

Five local tribes, the Muriwhenua, were celebrating a history-making precedent. The Waitangi Tribunal, newly empowered to settle claims arising from the 1840 treaty, had held that the local fishery belonged entirely to the five tribes. In victory the Muriwhenua adopted a generous stance. "We signed the Treaty as equal partners," said their leader Mat Rata, "and we're willing to share equally with the Crown: fifty-fifty." While negotiators struggled to work out new plans and the jubilant Muriwhenua assemblies looked ahead with realistic concern, many commentators reflected uneasiness. Nationwide, tribal claims to fisheries, forests, and public lands affected property worth an estimated 15 billion New Zealand dollars. That's in terms of the U.S. billion, a thousand millions; the British billion is a million millions.

Irene Neho, called "Tommy" for Tomboy, and I drove north for a special ritual in honor of the tribunal. A Pacific gale roared in, pummeled the windbreak trees, wailed around the meetinghouses. As she eased her rattletrap car around rain-slick corners, Irene told me of the life of fishing folk, how her husband could take his boat through the trickiest channels, sailing by the stars at night: "He was like the ancients. He used to fish with his great-grandfather William Savritsky." The Savritskys and other "Dallies"—Dalmatians, from the Adriatic—came to New Zealand a century ago. A welcome sign in Kaitaia reads *"Haere Mai / Dobro Dosli,"* and Maori and Slav mingle comfortably. Retired from the sea, Irene goes pig hunting on horseback, after the wild "Captain Cookers"—the nickname recalling the stock left by the explorer two centuries ago.

On the last high ground above Cape Reinga, the dignitaries angled their umbrellas warily into the uncompromising wind as a minister of the Ringatu Church chanted Scripture in classic Maori. Offshore, the waters of the Pacific and the Tasman met in swirls and welters of white. I remembered the story of Kupe told to me by Mat Rata: "When Kupe saw where the two oceans meet, he said, 'clearly this is the place of the gods.'" In the ancient Maori understanding, spirits of the dead journey northward through the island to this cape, make a last farewell, and descend to the realm of Hine-nui-te-Po, ancestress and sovereign lady of the dark. *Ka mate, ka mate! Ka ora, ka ora!*—It was death, it was death! It is life, it is life! □

FOLLOWING PAGES: Survivors from the days of Victoria keep a sunny outlook on a hillside of Wellington. Elsewhere, New Zealand's capital sports the look of later days, high rise à la mode.

PAUL CHESLEY / PHOTOGRAPHERS ASPEN

YVA MOMATIUK / JOHN EASTCOTT

Dashing figure of fitness: His Excellency the Governor-General of New Zealand, the Most Reverend Sir Paul Reeves jogs along a rampart of an ancient Maori fortress overlooking Auckland, the nation's metropolis. A devoted outdoorsman and the first archbishop to serve as governor-general, Sir Paul represents the Crown of Queen Elizabeth II.

Night prowler, a kiwi pokes for worms with a long beak often plunged to the hilt. Its call gave the kiwi its name. The towering kauri (opposite) survives in New Zealand only in remnant forests. This giant conifer, valued for masts and commercial gum, can live for centuries. Eventually decay rots its heartwood, and its hollow trunk often becomes a high-rise dwelling for bats.

WARREN JACOBS; DAVID MCVICKER /
PHOTOBANK IMAGE LIBRARY-NEW ZEALAND (OPPOSITE)

"Play the game, wear the gear." Lawn bowlers, all in white, honor the code even amid the rotten-egg aroma of Rotorua, tourist center of the North Island's volcanic belt. Half-timbered Tudor Towers, built as a spa, today houses a museum. Above: Steam boils up from geyser vents nearby. Local villagers still cook with heat in the ground.

FOLLOWING PAGES: Isolated cone of 8,261-foot Mount Egmont lures climbers to the island's west coast. Ash and mud spewed by the volcano in the past enrich surrounding dairy lands.

The South Island:
Gems of Ice and Jade

"We always had mud between our toes—shooting ducks, hunting mud eels." That was boyhood fun for young Bill Rowling at the family orchards near Tasman Bay. He grew up to a career in politics and now, in retirement, was fitting up a new bach at a cove on the bay, which fills the broad northern cleft of the South Island.

A bach (pronounced batch) is a holiday cottage, a place for casual weekends, a fixture of the good life in an uncrowded country. As we drove past coastal farms, Glen, Lady Rowling, recalled her parents' bach by a river—big Christmas dinners cooked on the wood-burning stove that also heated water for the tin bathtub on the veranda. "We used to have the most wonderful times!"

A buoyant holiday mood still marks the summers in the region called "top of the North." Yachts—small ones, usually—cruise on Queen Charlotte Sound or Tasman and Golden Bays. Families in their house trailers, known hereabouts as caravans, camp near the beaches around Nelson. Trampers take the coastal path in Abel Tasman National Park, or hike inland into the mountains. And residents here, like others farther south, grumble *(Continued on page 50)*

Silvery plume of Stirling Falls spills 505 feet into Milford Sound, steep-walled star of the South Island fjords; here tour boats linger for head-tilting views.

MacKinnon Pass unfurls a stunning view of glacier-gouged
Clinton Valley along the Milford Track, most famous trail in
a nation famed for its extensive trail system. A 33-mile
wilderness trek leading to Milford Sound, the track challenges
hikers with exhausting terrain, but such amenities as tea
breaks and overnight huts ease the burdens. So do the
chiming of bellbirds, the alpine skyline, the mossy, ferny bush
of Fiordland National Park. A scenic road, edged in places
with beech forest and tree ferns (left), cuts into Fiordland.
Heavy rainfall, averaging some 250 inches annually at
Milford Sound, nurtures the forests, including ferns unique
to the islands. New Zealand has adopted the leaves of one
indigenous species—the silver fern—as the national emblem.

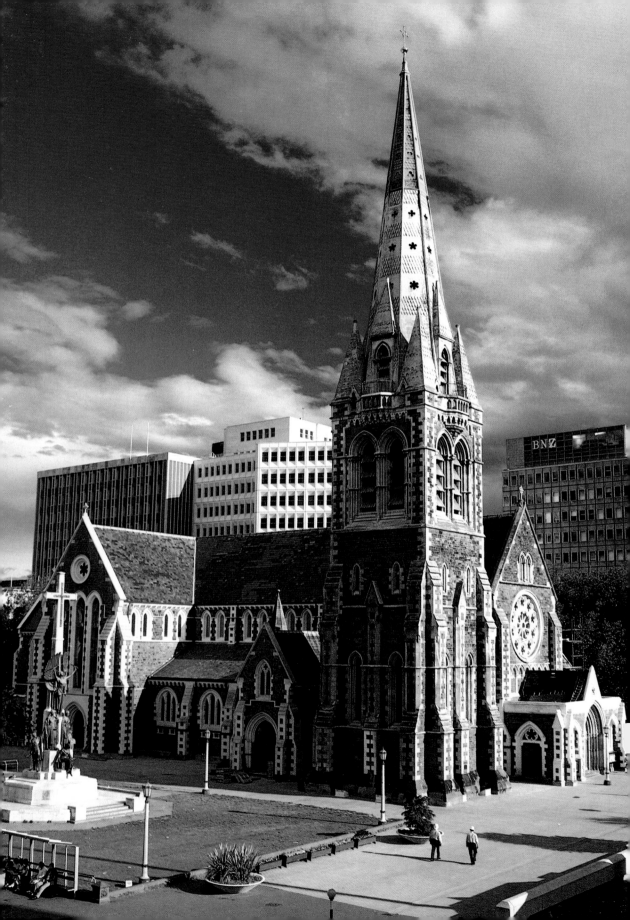

Gothic spire of the Cathedral Church of Christ dominates downtown Christchurch. Though the South Island's largest city has long been home to people of varied origins, the cathedral, a wealth of gardens, and the dreams of its Anglican founders perpetuate the image of "the most English city outside England." Rugby, born and bred in England's public schools, flourishes in New Zealand, a national passion. Above: Flanker Mike Brewer fights off tacklers as the national team, the All Blacks, downs Japan in Osaka in 1987. An international power in the sport, the All Blacks went on to win the world championship that year.

about North Islanders who go abroad instead of exploring the larger mainland of their own country. Often the gap between the two major islands seems far wider than Cook Strait.

Local pride, running deep throughout New Zealand, is especially vigorous in the South Island. Here ragged coasts and formidable mountains make for isolation, flavored now and then with a pinch of contrariness. West coast towns, I heard, have the best-developed cussedness of all, and I was disappointed when winter storms upset my plans to visit them. I made the most of Nelson's proverbial fine weather: brilliant sun, crisp air, gorse golden on the hillsides and lemons golden on a backyard tree beside the rotary clothes hoist. I watched a field hockey match where players outnumbered spectators (dogs included) and saluted the geographical center of New Zealand by hiking up Nelson's Botanical Hill on Sunday afternoon.

With about 45,000 people, Nelson puts the egalitarian life in perspective. A plumber, a teacher, a physician, a knight, and a truck driver may live side by side behind their hedges and fences, not necessarily as close friends but as friendly neighbors.

Leaving the gilded hills, I flew across snow-dusted peaks to the east coast and the South Island's metropolis. Christchurch styles itself "the most English city outside England," with century-old buildings in the Gothic style, with Cambridge and Oxford Terraces edging the Avon River. Oxford's Christ Church College gave the city its name. Here Japanese visitors, many of them newlyweds, photograph each other by the winding, silted-up little river, the dashing new town hall, or the wooden houses near the center of town that bear little resemblance to English counterparts.

"Wood flexes; brick falls down," merchant banker Mark Crawley said succinctly. "We have two or three quakes a year you can feel." Rising on the western horizon, the Southern Alps give the city a most un-English vista. Below the ranges, forcing them up, two gargantuan tectonic plates collide: from the west, the Indo-Australian Plate, and from the east, the Pacific Plate—whose opposite edge has scarred the face of California.

"I'm the only one who isn't dull!" cries the self-ordained Official Wizard of Christchurch, who entertains passersby with his speechifying in the city square before the Anglican Cathedral. "Is he really the only eccentric?" I asked a native. "The only visible one," I was told; "the rest are keeping it behind closed doors so they won't frighten the horses."

With 300,700 people—and seven youth orchestras—Christchurch is a lively place in many ways. The local polytechnic school sends experts abroad; the local branch of the Unisys Corporation exports computer software; the University of Canterbury welcomes visiting scholars. Still, says a resident Yank, "When I go out on a Sunday drive there're so few cars I think, 'California in 1910 must have been like this: unspoiled!'"

Identity is very much in the making, and the "Englishness" of

Christchurch is "really superficial," according to John and Ann Hercus. He directs the polytechnic school; she has been a cabinet minister and a member of Parliament; both are fifth-generation New Zealanders of Scottish stock. "Yes," she told me, "Christchurch was planned as an Anglican settlement, dominated by the English element. But half the people were Scots, Irish, Welsh, Swedes, Poles, plus our fair share of flipover from Australia, including a few convicts—it kind of ruined the plot."

"What we were taught about our past was monocultural and distorted," mused John. "Really," said Ann, "it was like the national dessert—you have tried a pavlova?" Named for the great ballerina, the pavlova is made with meringue and fresh fruit and slathers of whipped cream. "You see: bland and sickly sweet. We're learning that diversity can be more exciting."

As everyone points out, New Zealand is an intimate society. Citizens are quick to buttonhole their representatives. "Once," said Ann with a grin, "we were in a theater in London, and I felt a tap on my shoulder and a voice said, 'Ann Hercus! I've been wanting to speak to you about this chiropody bill!'—and that was in the middle of Act Two." Politicians do not have unlisted phone numbers. "I was minister of police, so anyone who had a grievance about the police might ring up. Quite a few ex-convicts did. And minister of women's affairs, which involved all the women plus all the men who disagreed with what we were doing."

"Not terribly mature" was Ann's verdict on relationships between men and women in Godzone. "There're deep stereotypes. 'Men are strong and masterful, women weak and subservient.' And men have a tendency to use their fists, against women as well as other men. We have a high level of violence; it looks horrific because we're a tiny country with a very efficient police. But there's a desire to try to tackle this question of violence." Ann concluded briskly: "If something's wrong, I have a Scottish Presbyterian instinct to fix it up!"

That's the essence of Dunedin, founded by Scottish settlers; its name is the Gaelic version of Edinburgh. "The Edinburgh of the South" almost surrounds its harbor on the southeast coast and covers the waterside hills, which turn golden in afternoon mist. "It's tough. It's stiff. It's sheer bloody-minded fuggosity," writes David Eggleston, a young poet with a no-holds-barred style, but he honors its strength: "the strength that comes from being cued-in, defiant, able to play at God." Its handsome old buildings include the First Church, Presbyterian, a Gothic landmark high on Bell Hill. Inside, up in the shadows, hangs the flag of the Otago Mounted Rifles—gold crown and green fern fronds on scarlet silk, with "Defence of Anzac" in its battle honors. Outside, I saw Samoan children romping on the grass.

A shop that morning offered "Thermal Underwear for Everyone and All Occasions." Another had a Mother's Day special ("with love"): items marked down from $1.55 to $1.29. And a classified ad in the *Otago Daily Times* read "LOST: Grey Fairisle Glove..." with a phone number.

"That person'll probably get that glove back," said Professor Charles Higham at the University of Otago, "the world's most southerly university." (Down Under is full of southernmosts.) He came from England in 1967 with the useful distinction of having played rugby for Cambridge. "It's an upper-class sport in England, very social," he admitted. "Here, as in Wales, it cuts across the entire spectrum. Some of the best players are farmers, great powerful men picking up sheep all day and tossing fence posts around." The All Blacks—the national team, clad in black uniforms—are New Zealand's particular heroes, a status enjoyed since the triumphant tour of Britain in 1905. But even the cult of rugby, like much else, has changed since the years "when all the cars were English."

Indeed, this land has forced change on its people since the days of its earliest settlers. Helen Leach, who has written a classic book entitled *1,000 Years of Gardening in New Zealand*, told me of the changes the first Polynesians had to make when their tropical plants, brought from warmer islands, blackened and shriveled under the uncanny veils of frost. Staples like kumara—sweet potato—wouldn't grow in the colder regions south of present-day Christchurch.

"People had to live as hunter-gatherers," she said, "learning which wild plants weren't toxic. They didn't want to give up living in villages—you can't carry heavy wood carvings around all the time—so they built great storehouses and frantically collected wild surplus in summer, like our mothers bottling fruit a generation ago."

"Quite possibly the South Island was the first settled area, around A.D. 900," added anthropologist Atholl Anderson. "On the archaeological evidence it had the high-protein resources, more seals and more of the flightless birds, especially the big moas." These were birds "in the size of dreams." The middle-size species, most often eaten, could glare at the hunter eye to eye. The largest, craning its neck to pluck a leaf, reached up 10 or 12 feet, and a slashing kick with 11-inch claws could have ripped a man apart. "Probably the hunters relied on snares," said Dr. Anderson, "and we've found dog skulls with powerful jaws like a dingo's. Dogs may have flushed the moa and bailed him up—held him at bay."

However they managed it, the Maori had hunted the moas to extinction before the white men came, and the North Island had already become the more populous. "We know the plants the moas ate," remarked Dr. Anderson; "our native hedges are made of those shrubs. Today the moas would survive in our suburbs." I never saw another suburban street without imagining a gigantic bird pacing along, pruning the hedge top, nibble by nibble, lifting its head warily when laundry flapped on the clothes hoist.

Dunedin's Otago Museum displays Maori and South Sea objects with notable flair and excellent lighting. I'm all in favor of good labels and lighting, especially when I'm admiring things I couldn't see anywhere else in the world, but I wouldn't alter any aspect of the Otago Early Settlers Museum in Dunedin. Its collection includes relics of pioneer days and some heroic retired steam locomotives. There is also the head of a noble ram, a triumph of taxidermy; set in the crown of the pate is a splendid silver snuff mill. Somber portraits crowd the walls: worthies who came in 1848 and after, stoic matrons and unyielding patriarchs, photographed in their best. I gazed up at them and thought of what one Dunedinite had said, about ways to have fun: "Well, I'm knitting myself a purple sweater."

Down on the southern coast I spent a tantalizing day at a grand wee island: Stewart, rugged, wooded, truly unspoiled. In Maori legend, the North Island is a fish that the demigod Maui hauled up from the deep; the South Island is his canoe, inverted and petrified; Stewart Island is the stone that anchored the canoe. Today it's home to about 520 humans. There are more kiwi birds than people, says Ron Tindal of the Department of Conservation. His office controls about 580 of the 674 square miles, and encourages year-round deer hunting. Exotic game species, like the notorious rabbit, have often become major pests Down Under. The seven white-tailed deer set loose on Stewart in 1908 have produced "lots and lots of relatives" that browse the bush to the danger point. It's tight forest, notes Ron, difficult to get through. Hikers who tramp the muddy trails allow a week or more for the 90-mile northern circuit.

Isolation comes into its own down here. It's wonderful for small children, but teenagers need more social life, according to Ann Pullen, whose husband was a fisherman here. Subantarctic water meets warmer currents in this region, and whalers and sealers once haunted these shores. Fishermen still do, but storms limit the fishing. An easterly was keeping the boats in harbor when I was there, so we inspected the spotless packing plant where men swap local gossip. We stopped at the spunky little museum, where I seized the chance to plug in lines on the switchboard of the old telephone exchange, recently retired from active duty. Outside the shoreline settlement, we squelched up muddy paths for hilltop views of coves where yachts can anchor. We identified crown fern, trailside under the thorny snarls known as lawyer vine. "It'll rip you!" warned Ann. Clouds were veiling the sky when we got to the airstrip for the daily (weather permitting) flight across 20-mile Foveaux Strait to the nation's southernmost city—Invercargill.

The tall plume of smoke from the aluminum smelter at Bluff Harbour, Invercargill's port, is a sign of hope; it means a payroll for about 1,300. "Without it," I was told, "there wouldn't be much over at Invercargill." Like Dunedin, Invercargill boomed in the gold rush of the 1860s and has waned recently. New Zealand, with plenty of hydroelectric power, lacks ore deposits. The smelter gets Australian alumina, from Queensland. Queensland gets New Zealanders looking for work. I saw some of them on regional TV news praising the Aussie weather and wages. About 600 Kiwi families a month were crossing the Tasman during my visit.

Some Americans have been crossing the Pacific annually for years to fish near Invercargill. "We have a thousand miles of good waters within 50 miles of town," Dr. Alfred Poole told me as we passed one trout stream after another. "Mostly brown trout here, browns and rainbows in the lakes." He's a cardiologist by profession, stone carver by choice, who searches high-country rivers and fault zones for jade with his neighbor Russell Beck. Russ has written the book on New Zealand greenstone, the treasure of the Maori.

Beyond worked-out gold zones and ghost towns we came to a beach where huge dollops of gray-green rock curved down into the breakers. This was argillite, fine-grained stone that the Maori used for adzes. Fire-reddened flakes marked a prehistoric toolmaking site. Farther along the beach Alf and Russ, hammers in hand, saw with disgust that the tide had already covered a boulder they wanted. We turned to hunting green garnet in the beach cobbles and gravel. "It's called hydrogrossular garnet, very rare," said Alf. How rare? "Oh, one bit in every hundred thousand tons. Russ can spot them." A hill above the strand caught my eye; there two youngsters were "sledding" country style—on a big frond of green leaves.

Back in town, I saw the lovely free-form jades that Alf and Russ have worked: "fondle pieces." I saw ancient pieces that the Maori carved, pendants and chisel blades and clublike weapons called *mere*, treasures of the museum that Russ directs; and I saw a boulder that nature alone had shaped, translucent pale blue-green jade flecked with white—a swirl of mountain river struck by magic into stone.

"To the Maori, jade was alive," said Russ. "The jade they found in a river held the spirit of a fish." The jade here is nephrite, an extremely tough natural material, formed under extreme pressure. "It expresses the geological history of the earth," said Russ. Now, for me, a dark green pendant I bought evokes New Zealand, and in the carved swirls of jade I see the curves of young fern fronds in the North and the ageless somber forests of the South.

"In most countries," says a well-traveled friend, "you visit a beauty spot, and then you go on, and you come to another one. In New Zealand the beauty just goes on, mile after mile." Especially in the high country of the South Island. I asked a veteran coach driver there what single spot the tourists liked best. "Ah, Mount Cook," he replied, "she spellbounded them when she came out!" Much of the time she stays in, in the long white cloud that often cloaks the highlands. But on one afternoon of diamond air and sun I had an unforgettable view of the summit and bladelike ridges of the "cloud piercer," crowning the high valleys where shrinking glaciers send their meltwater purling down from the snow zone. Such scenes may touch the most agnostic hearts. "I'm not a religious man," said a young ski buff, "but when you see the mountains and snow you think, 'Someone has been rather clever.'"

One of the cleverest touches is the placement of water. S-shaped Lake Wakatipu zigzags for 48 miles between the ranges, including the aptly named Remarkables with their glistening peaks rising along the lakeshore. At Queenstown, an old mining town and today a Southland vacation center offering splendid views of the lake and mountains, I boarded the old steamer *Earnslaw* for a voyage through country that seemed, at first glance, totally undeveloped. Beyond splotches of gold where someone had planted larches or poplars, hills had the color of deerskin. Our black trail of coal smoke thinned below shining summits. Decent roads crawled in to lakeside as late as the 1930s; two stations—as Kiwis and Aussies call ranches—still rely solely on boats. Beyond the valleys, great breakers of mountain rose into jagged white crests.

At Mount Nicholas Station, old hand Ron Collins gave a short course in the most romantic of topics: sheep. He recited the familiar joke of the Yankee tourist: Told that the country has 65 million sheep, the visitor says, "I've seen the whole blank-blank lot except three." Mount Nicholas runs about 26,000 wool producers, and we saw only a handful. Five men, with six or seven dogs apiece, were bringing the flocks down from the high range, where one sheep needs three and a half acres of native tussock grasses, to winter range, where as many as eight can live on an acre of fertilized pasture. In the good old days, it's said, "the sheep ate all the grass we could grow, and Britain ate all the sheep."

Dogs are all-important. Of border collie stock, mainly, they vary in looks and style. A "strong-eyed" dog controls the sheep with a stare of dominance. A "huntaway" is a "very noisy, boisterous fellow," said Ron, that relies on barking. A "handy" has traits of both. All "appear to understand swearing better than anything else." Ron's black mutt fidgeted beside him until a signal sent him streaking off with a *wooof* of excitement. Tail streaming, he hurdled a gate and sped away to a hillside where he cut behind a cluster of creamy dots and woofed them into a gallop. They charged into the home paddock and Ron took one for a shearing. In three minutes his electric shears zipped off the fleece, gray outside as a glacier top but creamy underneath. Ron straightened up: "Anybody want a haircut?"

Our wool samples tucked away, we raced sundown at 13 knots while a white-haired pianist belted out old tunes on an old Canadian upright—"Tipperary," "Maori Farewell," "Click Go the Shears."

Towheaded youngsters sang with their elders or beat time with ice-cream cones.

I sampled jetboating in the gray gorges of the Shotover River. A Kiwi invention for shallow streams, a jetboat with a dozen adults wedged in draws 18 inches at rest. Planing, it needs only 4. A grate in the flat bottom inhales water, which is expelled through a nozzle for steering and propulsion—up to about 40 miles per hour, officially. It felt like Mach 2, hurtling through shadowy narrows, whooosh-*whump*-whoooosh! over gravel bars, spinning through sun-bright spray in a Hamilton turn—full circle at full speed within the boat's own length. Passengers' squeals, I decided, deflect it from overhanging rock. Ashore, taking off my life jacket, I heard a blond girl from Auckland tell a balding Yank: "That's what we do when we don't want to do something thrilling."

Uncluttered, untamed country is a thrill in its own right for many visitors, especially the Japanese. Queenstown, with its gold-rush relics and flight-seeing excursions, had been enjoying a tourism boom. Still, as I was told by some Kiwis (and some Aussies), foreigners may find life in Godzone laid-back in ways they hadn't expected. "Tourism won't succeed here," one New Zealander told me, "until people stop being so lackadaisical about it." The remark reminded me of the day when a hotel porter volunteered to flag down the airport coach for me. He duly waved as the vehicle approached; the driver cheerfully waved back—and drove on.

Food and wine have become popular objects of reviews and critiques. Down Under inherited the British-is-best style of cuisine, but the gray-meat-and-two-veggies cult is waning. New Zealand's wine-growers are fine-tuning their vintages. Food is good—Bluff oysters are delectable—and cooking is ambitious.

On a Wellington menu artichoke hearts "with quark, beetroot and cucumber" caught my eye—too late, unfortunately, to investigate quark. A breakfast card in Invercargill included croissants. I ordered one. The waitress, a student working on vacation, seemed torn between professional briskness and human concern. "I saw one in the kitchen," she confided, "but I think it's stale. I think you would be happier with toast." The toast and jam were fine, but that's not why I remember the incident so happily. Service may be unhurried, but it's often as engaging as a spearmint milkshake.

Racetracks excepted, hustle is usually as unwelcome as change. "New Zealanders rather relish competition," I was told, "but they don't like change." Older people tended to endorse that view, I found; younger people, however, often had an agenda for change, as did women and, of course, the Maori.

In an all-time flub, a reference book of 1911 called the fjords of the southwest "grand but commercially useless." The region has all-world scenery, with full value for visitors; Milford Sound expects 2,000 a day in summer. I took a coach tour from Queenstown with a driver who seemed to know all the quirks. He told of a town where moonshine is legally sold in the hardware store, as paint stripper. And of Mossburn, with 350 people and four rugby teams. We crossed open terrain where tussock waved in the wind like the mane of a galloping palomino; we had scones and tea at sun-dappled Lake Te Anau. From manuka scrub, called tea trees because Captain Cook brewed tea from the leaves, we entered beech forest and Fiordland National Park: "One of the last great wilderness areas, nearly three million acres if you want to get yourself lost."

A New Zealand traffic jam stopped us: a roadful of sheep, broken up by a horseman with seven black dogs and happily photographed by a Japanese couple. Between anecdotes about avalanches, the driver praised the safety of the Milford Track for bushwalking: "no tigers, no grizzly bears . . . no crocodiles, no snakes." In a hiker's heaven of a nation, this 33-mile trail is a wilderness route that requires reservations made in advance—far in advance for a group tour with a guide. It also demands clothes for changeable weather.

From cloud we had passed into drizzle, then into wet snow. Below the tunnel at Homer Pass the driver put on chains— "I'm gonna have a go"—and inched up in bottom gear, chains whumping and clinking. Snow traced every ledge and crevice on the dark cliffs above us. Every beech leaf became a petal of white. Spiky leaves of native flax doubled under the load; ferns sagged and splayed like white starfish.

At Milford Sound the downpour was chill rain. "Weather's a little indifferent today, folks," conceded the host on the cruise boat. Instant cataracts gained volume as we eased past. "You couldn't see the waterfalls any better." This dogged make-the-best-of-it commentary stirred my admiration as much as it amused me. "What do you tell the poor souls who get a sunny day?" I asked a crewman, and he was too polite to answer. Mitre Peak, a knife-edged pinnacle in the travel posters, slid by on the southern shore, blurred like black gauze seen through gray gauze. Finally the boat began to pitch as waves from the Tasman Sea surged into the entrance of the sound, and I knew why Captain Cook had kept his ships well offshore. Weather comes from the Indian Ocean past southern Australia to strike this coast with enormous waves, said the crewman, a veteran of crayfishing. "The sea turns upside down along here." We turned back, rolling, and made our way to the pier.

In due course our coach made it safely through the snow. The driver switched on his taped music, a tinkling music-box serenade, and two pretty Japanese girls sang along with it, softly. The song was "Waltzing Matilda."

Even to foreigners it evokes Australia, and I always feel like singing it when I'm on my way there. □

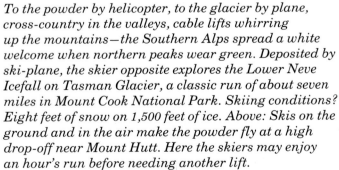

*To the powder by helicopter, to the glacier by plane,
cross-country in the valleys, cable lifts whirring
up the mountains—the Southern Alps spread a white
welcome when northern peaks wear green. Deposited by
ski-plane, the skier opposite explores the Lower Neve
Icefall on Tasman Glacier, a classic run of about seven
miles in Mount Cook National Park. Skiing conditions?
Eight feet of snow on 1,500 feet of ice. Above: Skis on the
ground and in the air make the powder fly at a high
drop-off near Mount Hutt. Here the skiers may enjoy
an hour's run before needing another lift.*

ANDRIS APSE

LLOYD PARK

Sheepherders coax a flock of
merinos across a stream near
Lake Pukaki to shearing
sheds and summer grazing
lands. Often farmers carry
dogs to pasture on bikes (left),
keeping the animals fresh
for their arduous chores. At the
annual Royal Agricultural
Society Show in Christchurch
(right), rams sit up as judges
check health and posture
and the color, length,
and strength of the wool.

FOLLOWING PAGES: A new
day bids rise and shine to
dozing pleasure craft in Queen
Charlotte Sound near Picton.

WARREN JACOBS

YVA MOMATIUK / JOHN EASTCOTT

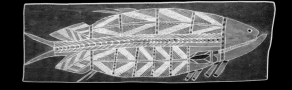

WEATHERED MONOLITHS, THE OLGAS JUT FROM DESERT PLAINS IN CENTRAL AUSTRALIA.

AUSTRALIA

The Making of a Homeland

TOP LEFT: ABORIGINAL BARK PAINTING IN X-RAY STYLE DEPICTS A BARRAMUNDI FISH

Land of Long Vistas

"I love a sunburnt country," writes an Australian poet. The harsh outback, dry as a sunstruck bone, fascinates Australians—but four-fifths of them live within 50 miles of the coast. About a third of the land has too little water for economic use. Yet Aborigines found a living in even the most desolate terrain. Six states and the Northern Territory grew out of British colonies; some of the following chapters cross state boundaries to explore distinctive landscapes and lifeways in the dry interior, the stormy north, and the crowded eastern fringe. Emu and kangaroo in the nation's coat of arms (above) exemplify the marvelous wildlife that evolved here, in nearby New Guinea—and nowhere else.

ABOVE: ILLUSTRATION BY PAUL M. BREEDEN

66

INDONESIA

TIMOR

INDIAN OCEAN

KIMBERLEY REGION

Broome

Christmas Creek

Great Sandy Desert

Port Hedland

Marble Bar

Onslow

North West Cape

Hamersley Range

PILBARA

WESTERN

Gibson Desert

AUSTRALIA

Lake Carnegie

Wiluna

Geraldton

Gwalia

Kalgoorlie

NAMBUNG N.P.

Perth

Bunbury

Esperance

Margaret River

PORONGURUP N.P.

Pemberton

Albany

INDIAN OCEAN

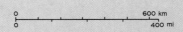

600 km

400 mi

River red gum trees trace an underground watercourse in arid Simpsons Gap National

Central Australia:
The Dry Interior

Park; an ancient stream carved the gorge in the MacDonnell Ranges near Alice Springs.

"Over there's the camel polo field, and the cricket pitch," said the bloke in the old felt hat. Over there behind the pub was a flattish patch of dusty red earth and red pebbles, the cracked stuff that gave the continent's Red Centre its nickname. It was unsuitable for every sport in the world except the deadpan leg-pulling of the Australian bush—the hard, dry humor for a hard, dry land, as an old-timer put it. I've known Australians long enough to recognize a sporting challenge.

"How about croquet?" I parried. "Ah yeah, croquet," said Jeff Barnard; "players in starched white linen." I liked that: the uniform for green lawns in placid suburbs. Out here the local style ran to dusty boots, out-at-the-knee work pants, sweat-stained hats. We were about as close to the middle of the continent as you can get, out in the MacDonnell Ranges near a ghost town. When Alice Springs got too citified for Gary and Elaine Bohning, they had moved out here to revive the old Arltunga hotel, locally famous as the loneliest pub in the scrub. Gary had cleared the "camel polo field" for tourists to park in. Tourists had been thin on the ground,

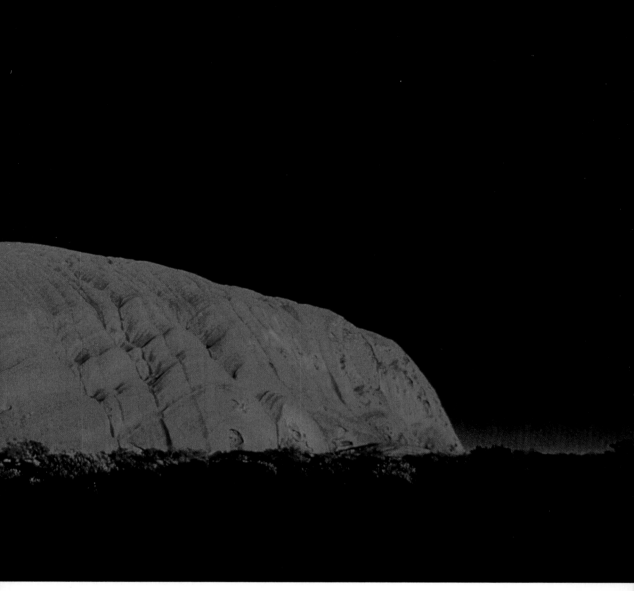

*Powerful symbol of the red heart of Australia, Uluru, or Ayers Rock,
looms vermilion at sunrise. Iron in the rock oxidizes, giving it its
famous rusty hue; shifts in light and shadow highlight gullies and
crevices, contributing to its many moods and colors. Part of Uluru
National Park, it attracts 250,000 visitors each year, most of them
in winter; summer temperatures exceed 100° F. Climbers—Aborigines
call them* minga rama, *crazy ants—attempt a steep morning trek to
the top of the 1,142-foot monolith (left). Erosion on the hiking trails,
as well as on the rock itself, arouses growing concern. Aborigines
have performed ceremonies at Uluru for many generations, probably
for millennia; to them the rock remains sacred.*

like raindrops, but Australians specialize in turning frustration to sardonic fun. We sat around joking over good cold beer.

From camel tactics we strayed to legendary monsters and then to the topic of painting. The time-gnawed red stone and timeless light of this region have inspired some of Australia's best artists, including Sir Sidney Nolan and the great watercolorist Albert Namatjira. My companions had a bushman's eye for terrain and, like many Australians, an impressive knowledge of painting. The barkeeper was ripe for a long discussion of Picasso's influence.

From art the talk turned to mining. The town of Arltunga had thrived on gold from 1897 through 1903, but this gold rush, it's said, was "the rush that slowed." Gary and Elaine do a bit of fossicking, old-fashioned prospecting. They showed me Elaine's "Christmas nugget," a four-ounce holiday find, and a lump of white quartzite with a gleaming outcrop the size of a bush fly, one wing askew. "Gold's cranky," said Gary; "she hides from you."

He guided me about the town, explaining that "Water was always the problem here—water and isolation." On a dusty side road he pointed out a dog track: "Running. A dingo, and he was chasing a euro." The scuffy pad marks of the hill kangaroo and the claw-tipped spoor of the wild dog ended on rock. A crow shrieked nearby like an unoiled hinge: *aaark ock arrrrk-arrrrrk*. We stopped at a mass of rusting machinery, tons of it. Men and horses had dragged it from the railhead at Oodnadatta, struggling six months to cover less than 400 miles. The hopeful entrepreneur finally had it on site—just as the rush was petering out. "I reckon it broke his heart same as it broke everyone else's," said Gary. "It was a very hard field."

Hard. It's a word that comes up over and over again in Australia, especially in the outback, the huge dry interior, almost 70 percent of the country. Roughly, this area averages less than 20 inches of rain a year, but the figure masks wild variations. I visited an area in Queensland that had baked for six years; then the rains came—on the winds of a cyclone. I heard about a farmer in New South Wales who was celebrating the bicentenary with his first good wheat crop in 11 years. In irrigation country near the Murray River, I met a man who remembered moving from the drought-parched Riverina district: "I was a boy of five. When the horse and wagon clattered over a bridge, I was scared. I asked my granddad, 'What's that?' He said, 'That's called a river, son. It's water. And if we had had any at home we wouldn't be here now!'"

Rivers shown on maps may have no water at all. If a stream's "coming down," rain has fallen upcountry and water is rushing along, probably in torrents. Often an inland river runs upside down; that is, you see the sandy bed but not the water slinking along under it. The Todd River at Alice Springs is a good example.

"The farther inland you Americans went, the better it got," one Australian said to me. I thought of Kentucky pastures, Iowa cornfields. "The farther inland we went, the worse it got." Understandably, most Australians live close to the coast, and much of my journey took me to coastal cities, but any acquaintance with the interior leaves an indelible sense of space, dryness, emptiness. Reddish-brown country, scruffy with scrub, vanishes in distant dust. Vacant streaks of road appear, meet, run toward nothing visible. Gray-white rims of salt outline wastes of yellow gray, blotches of desolation. A chain of salt "lakes" curves for 1,200 miles across the continent, and once or twice in a lifetime bursts of rainfall may leave one or two of them brimming with water.

An Aussie truck driver sees the interior as "mobs of nothing." An Aborigine of traditional belief sees the land very differently. "*Epama epam*—nothing is nothing," one has said. Stony plain or mountain forest, sand dune or swamp, every portion of Australia had its own identity, its resources, its human owners and its sacred meaning. At one point in the so-called Red Centre these two angles of vision intersect. This is the huge domelike monolith famous as Ayers Rock or, for many generations, as Uluru.

For many foreigners and most Australians, this natural monument symbolizes the continent as the Sydney Opera House stands for civilization. People come by the planeful or coachload, to climb the rock, to drive or hike around the base, to take photographs at sunset. Then cloud may give the rock a somber purple glow, or dust a brilliant orange. I saw a hue like old gold, and fleeting ashes of rose. "Film can't take that up," remarked my companion, Alex Bogusiak, an official of Uluru National Park at the time. He has seen the rock glistening and sinister after rain, or streaming with waterfalls, or looming above a silver sheen in the grasses under a full moon. A shadow band rose like storm surge as the sun went down.

When Alex drove a park Land Cruiser from Uluru to the Olgas, a jumble of domes that have the ancient name Kata Tjuta—"many heads"— he commented on the abundance of termites and the hardness of their mounds. Along the 14 miles of unpaved track he veered off into the scrub occasionally to show how life-forms adapt here.

At a young mulga tree he flexed an upward-pointed leaf. If it rains, such leaves funnel water down the stems to the branches, the trunk, the roots. "Rain on this soil—it's like trying to get flour wet." Soil temperatures in summer reach 140° or 150°F. He pointed out the grasses called spinifex, which thrive in such conditions; apologized for not finding grubs at a witchetty bush; and let me taste nectar from the greenish yellow blossom of a shrub called honey grevillea. Witchetty grubs and spinifex seeds and nectar—valued foods for the Aborigines here. "They never starved," said Alex, "but in summer you limit your exertions to the absolute minimum." We spotted a brown falcon as we climbed a scree slope. Seen from the Olgas, Uluru seemed larger than ever. It needs distance to impose its full bulk, two miles in width. "It was here a long time before the first human foot walked on earth," Alex said softly, "and it will be here long after we're gone."

That's the perspective of geology. Aboriginal people speak of the time when Ancestral Beings created all the features of the land: mountains, springs, claypans. These Beings had the forms of humans and animals and plants. They traveled throughout the land, performing marvels. The paths they took are recalled in song and story, retraced on journeys; the sites of their deeds are known and named; and the creative essence of the Ancestor lives in a particular feature—a rock, perhaps, or a clump of plants. Thanks to a British anthropologist, the source of this ancient belief is known in English as the Dreamtime, or Dreaming. The term's a misnomer but, like other mistakes, seems established beyond repair.

Traditional owners of Uluru once again hold title to the land and care for its sacred sites. They sell artifacts made of mulga wood and kangaroo sinew and spinifex resin. They also show a film, professionally made under their direction; I watched it, moved by its feeling for the land, saddened by its tales of land and lives lost to the whites, amused by its fast-forward scenes of scurrying tourists. It left many visitors shaken and sobered.

"Historically, it's important," explained anthropologist Susan Woenne-Green, an employee of the resident community; "the mob here is really used to being done in. It's hard to convince visitors of the religious context here." (By "mob," she meant the traditional owners; in Australian English, a mob is simply a group—of citizens or birds or livestock.)

Admiring the shapely mass of Uluru from the air, I thought that it helps explain why Aborigines considered only the natural as sacred. A low-altitude flight northeast revealed one landmark after another. At an oasis called Palm Valley, cabbage palms and cycads— the many-fronded plants that artists surround dinosaurs with—cling to life, collecting water seeping through tilted sandstone. In an age with a wetter climate, such trees covered most of the Red Centre. Casting purple shadows, the long red ridges of the MacDonnell Ranges lay cusped like gargantuan molar teeth, fossil remains of mountains. Then the supersecret white structures of the U.S. base at Pine Gap gave an early warning of the electronic present.

"It's the *centre* of Australia, It's the *place* that's really *swinging* . . . Alice leads the way. . . ." Amplifiers blared this theme song through the Todd Mall at Alice Springs, past shops like In-jean-ious. In the town's central business district you find Kentucky Fried Chicken next to the Centre for Aboriginal Artists and Craftsmen. With about 24,000 residents—including some 6,000 Aborigines—the Alice is the largest town for 400 miles, source of supplies for remote cattle stations and streams of tourists. I was there for its celebrated annual blowout, the Henley-on-Todd Regatta.

I found a patch of shade under a coolibah tree, a wonderfully leafy eucalypt, by a sign for "shark-infested waters." Naturally, in October, the riverbed doesn't float anything. For the major competition, contestants assemble inside bottomless racing shells—eight bodies per boat. They sprint down the course, around a marker, and back through the loose sand. Let a single racer get out of step and the whole shebang may sink in profane confusion. One mob turned its hard-charging skiff into a 16-legged sideways kayak, and the crowd guffawed. The base at Pine Gap had entered a crew. "The Yanks have been training for months," warned the announcer. "Up early every morning, running for miles. Our lads have been drinking a lot of beer." The Yanks, well synchronized, did cross the finish line first. In the high traditions of international yachting, and greatly to the satisfaction of the spectators, they were disqualified for running a boat oversize at the waterline.

"You've got to have your own fun in these places," I was told one night under the gum trees. Pat and Norma Brennan had put some extra steaks and sausages on the backyard barbecue and invited me over to meet Mrs. Pearl Price Powell. Pearl came to the Alice in World War I, at age six, when her father managed the telegraph station that helped link Australia with London. She told me about the town of two houses in 1917, and the end of a six-year drought in 1919, and mustering cattle in 1922, and the six weeks required for mail delivery by camelback. She still has a scar from the ritual that made her "blood sister" to an Aboriginal girl many years ago.

In recent years the Alice has been growing rapidly. Australians come because they like to see the sights of their own country; and some stay, enjoying the comforts of civilization and the isolation of the bush. (Bush, in Australia, can be almost anything nonurban.) Mayor Leslie Oldfield came to the Alice in 1969 and "I'm still here. I was a secretary—where else could I end up as mayor?"

Bob Liddle, elected alderman in his hometown in 1983, made history as the first candidate of part-Aboriginal descent to win a seat in local government in the Northern Territory. The Alice isn't a racist town, in his opinion, but it's conservative—ultraconservative, in lots of ways. That's typical of the Territory, say other Australians, but the place has its innovative side.

The wavy lines that suggest a watercourse, or a serpent track, in traditional art now form a logo for Imparja Television, the first Aborigine-owned TV station. It began broadcasting in 1988, showing a cricket match played in Perth between Australia and New Zealand. It planned locally produced programs in Aboriginal languages for communities deep in the bush. There, I was told, the elders don't think children should spend too much time watching shows like "Miami Vice." The dry interior is an enormous place, an arduous place, but part of a shrinking world. □

PHILIP QUIRK / WILDLIGHT; © JEAN-PAUL FERRERO / AUSCAPE (ABOVE)

Closing for the kill, a dingo runs down a grey kangaroo in the southeastern mountain country. For perhaps 8,000 years dingoes, wild dogs of Asian origin, ranged the continent; they still abound in the interior and the far north. A fence, running 6,000 miles from the southern coast almost to the Gulf of Carpentaria, bars the dingoes from prime semiarid pastoral lands. A boundary rider, with tame best friend, inspects a reach of fence in a dry corner of New South Wales. His truck mounts protective "roo bars," standard in rural areas. Kangaroos amazed European explorers. Captain Cook's men, hoping to capture a specimen, loosed greyhounds on one. Helped by high grass, the roo outsped the hounds, unlike the luckless leaper above.

Hurtling across tableland of the Northern Territory, road trains—heavy-duty trucks pulling trailers—haul cattle 600 miles to an eastern port. Since the 1960s routes like this one, called beef roads, have stitched two-thirds of the country and transformed the economy. Powder-fine dust billows as a vehicle crosses the 50,000-square-mile Simpson Desert. A trucker (below) bathes at a portable oasis—under his rig; a desert sign warns: "Do not spit. You might need it."

GÜNTHER DEICHMANN

Outback outpost: Barrow Creek, whose year-round residents all gather here for a town portrait, straddles the Stuart Highway, main north–south artery of central Australia. The settlement began as a telegraph relay station, to keep dots and dashes pulsing across 1,800 miles of cable strung from the bottom of the continent to the top. Before 1872 a message to London took ten weeks by ship; the Overland Telegraph Link cut that time to two days. The two-lane highway traces the overland route; Aussies celebrated the blacktopping of the final section in 1987.

*Clean lines and clear colors define the desert near
Alice Springs (above). Imported in the 1860s, camels
ferried explorers and freight; now they carry tourists on
desert safaris. Northward toward the tropics, where the
Katherine River flows (opposite), the climate changes.
Visitors boat past galleries of Aboriginal rock art on the
walls of Katherine Gorge in Australia's winter and spring,
the dry season here. Monsoon, oppressive humidity, and
heat mark the wet—November through March.*

Egrets swoop above grasses and sedges greened, and waters swollen, by tropical

The Arc of Storms

storms in Kakadu National Park, home to about a third of Australia's bird species.

In the springtime days of October and November the tropic heat builds along with the soaring cumulus, thunderbolts crackling across the skies, clouds billowing at times as high as Everest piled upon Everest. Then come the summer months of the season known as the Wet, when monsoon rains saturate the northern coasts. Above the wavering southern margin of this rainfall zone is historic cattle country, mining country, and a state of mind.

"We're North Australians—not Queenslanders, Territorians, or Western Australians," says cattleman Peter Murray of Broome. Murray believes his region supports the "worn-out" states far to the south. "In northern Australia you can still make your way."

Darwin the Damned, as the port used to be known, made its way through squalid early years with the help of a gold rush, while residents soothed sand fly bites and other sorrows drinking grog made with cheap gin, kerosene, Worcestershire sauce, ginger, and sugar. It's still a place to go pub-crawling and to enjoy tropical lunacies—go troppo, as they say. Here you can arm-wrestle a Darwin stubby, a beer bottle that holds more *(Continued on page 90)*

*David Malangi of Ramingining, one of Arnhem
Land's best-known artists, completes a painting
that evokes the Dreaming, or Creation, of his clan.
Ancestral figures called the Djan'kawu Sisters
made a well and caught a catfish—central image
of this panel—at a site where they gave birth to the
people of the country. Malangi has singed and
scraped his length of eucalyptus bark and
flattened it under stones. He grinds his red and
yellow ocher pigments in a stone mortar of ancient
type, but paints with sable brushes and uses
plastic bowls for water as a matter of convenience.*

DAVID ROBERT AUSTEN (ALL)

Daubed with ocher and clay, clansmen from western
Arnhem Land brandish spears as they dance. One at left
grips a woomera, or spear-thrower, which increases the
missile's range and impact. This device appeared in rock art
of the region some 6,000 years ago—and served warriors
guarding the coast in World War II. In the rock painting
opposite, a hunter hiding behind a bundle of long grass has
fatally wounded an emu with a multi-barbed spear. The
artist recorded the successful hunt, perhaps 15,000 years ago,
at Mount Brockman in what is now Kakadu Park.

GEORGE CHALOUPKA; © JEAN-PAUL FERRERO / AUSCAPE (ABOVE)

than half a U.S. gallon. At the posh new casino, planned for high rollers from Brunei and Hong Kong and Singapore, you can sit under the palms and watch the sunset over the Arafura Sea, a miracle of turquoise water.

Tropical storms may strike the coast anywhere between, roughly, Onslow in the west and Townsville in the east. Luckily, there're few towns for targets. In 1897 a cyclone smashed up Darwin; replacement buildings were bombed to splinters by the Japanese in World War II. At Christmas in 1974 Cyclone Tracy demolished almost everything in the rebuilt town. Rebuilt yet again, the Top End port is looking far afield for an expanding role in international trade.

In the downtown mall, vendors with delicate Asian features blend iced milkshakes with your choice of tropical fruit: papaya, pineapple, banana. Others serve spicy dishes from Thailand, Laos, Malaysia. "When people down south get meat pies," remarked a friend, "here they get saté." Here, unmistakably, the Far East is the Near North.

Looking south as far as Hobart, Darwin sees 16 million customers. Northward an equal distance, it sees 300 million. The capital of the Northern Territory is closer to Jakarta, Indonesia's capital, than to Adelaide, closer to Manila than to Melbourne. A woman from Montenegro via London summed up a trend: "We're almost about to become cosmopolitan in Darwin."

At the Museum of Arts and Sciences in Darwin I explored an aspect of life that is supremely insular. Australia can claim the planet's least cosmopolitan land mammals. She shares oddities of her unique fauna only with New Guinea, which formed part of the continent until 8,000 years ago. Over millions of years of isolation, scientists say, marsupials occupied the niches the land offered. Koalas and kangaroos are almost trademarks, but more than a hundred other species survive—marsupial mice, possums, wombats like oversize badgers.

In the museum another Peter Murray, a naturalized Aussie from Oregon, introduced me to stranger species that had vanished over the past 40,000 years. His most fearsome specimen was the massive skull of the "marsupial lion," *Thylacoleo carnifex.* "Here're attachments for big powerful muscles. Two big premolars—they're carnassial teeth that worked like bolt cutters; they could shear bone." Peter and art specialist George Chaloupka have identified one of the region's ancient rock paintings as a likeness of this predator. He brought out the great toe of a forefoot with a razor-sharp claw. "These were powerful animals, about the size of a leopard, probably ambush hunters. Probably good at climbing trees." So much for the idea of an artist studying his subject from a strong high branch. Then Peter showed me the skull of a so-called marsupial tapir and pointed out the marks of crocodile teeth on the bone.

I remembered those specimens one evening in Kakadu National Park, east of Darwin. I was out at a remote billabong with Dave Lindner, environmental manager for the park's Aboriginal owners, the Gagudju Association. Dave takes game now and then for the elders. He loaded his double-barreled shotgun and flushed some mag-pie geese. One of the big birds struck the water near shore and float-ed along as a breeze roughed up cat's-paw riffles. Other ripples appeared, converging on the goose against the wind.

"Crocs," said Dave; "not very big—ten or twelve feet." The crimson western sky was darkening. He got out a flashlight. Five or six pairs of eyes shone blood-ruby in its beam. A wider V of ripples was moving in, steadily. "There's the big one." The dreadnought croc collected its prize as more and more red glints answered the light: eight or ten by the far shore, others quartering the center, thou-sands of jaws snapping at my nerves when a twig cracked under Dave's boot. As they say, the croc's the boss animal up here.

When Dave turned homeward, the headlights caught a din-go standing alert at the edge of woodland. Dave braked. The dog tossed his head in a "No Worries!" style and eased into the dark. Dave drove on, describing the thunderstorms that precede and follow the Wet. He has seen a couple of thousand lightning bolts in an hour. "You can read a paper by them—flash and flash and f-l-a-s-h." Once he had a pet dingo that tried to bite the lightning, leaping into the humid air and snapping at the brightness. "You do wonder what's in their minds."

On a morning round we stopped at a spectacular vista, across grassland to Nourlangie Rock, the great sandstone massif that ap-pears in the movie *"Crocodile" Dundee*. I was astonished to learn that this scenery is new, or renewed. Conservation work restored it after water buffalo, imported in the 1800s, had spread across the north and grazed the land bare. "When buffalo numbers were higher in this country," said Dave, "it was either a mudhole or dust bowl." Another conservation battle was raging during my visit and after. It focused on Coronation Hill, a mound of rusty-buff sandstone in the South Alligator Valley. Here, in an area already known for gold and uranium, geologists had found signs of platinum and palladium. The venture was led by BHP—the Broken Hill Proprietary Co. Ltd, greatest of Australian corporations. The day I was there crews had cut platforms on the hillside; diamond drills were in place; an envi-ronmental impact statement was being prepared.

Fighting the project were the greenies and the Jawoyn. Green-ies are conservationists; they feared the threat of pollution. The Jawoyn, traditional owners of the area, say the powerful Dreamtime creator Bula lives underground here. If disturbed, he will bring di-saster—fires, floods, earthquakes. Federal authority would decide if the area would be mined or become part of Kakadu Park. Like Uluru, Kakadu is an Australian oddity, a national park administered by federal officials. At both sites the Commonwealth returned land to Aboriginal ownership and then leased it back for park purposes.

Other "national" parks are created and run by a state or territory.

BHP personnel assured me that they were avoiding sacred sites and would safeguard the environment. A geologist maneuvered a Land Cruiser up an outcrop that would challenge a euro. It gave the best view of the valley, rock ramparts veiled in gray-green scrub. It seemed pristine—except where dust-white ramps slashed the hillside.

"You don't come here to see engineering feats," Dave said tersely later. We saw an array of haunting landscapes: the great escarpment edging the Arnhem Land Plateau; sluggish rivers, low from the long Dry; pools full of red lotus blossoms. Near the lookout called Koongarra Saddle, cracks in the sandstone give outcrops an uncanny resemblance to temple ruins of India. Elsewhere, under protective overhangs, rock paintings record changes in animal and human life that may cover 35,000 years, according to George Chaloupka. The world's oldest crayons, dark purple hematite stubs used 30,000 years ago, come from a site that Dave Lindner spotted in 1972.

Nourlangie Rock holds marvels. Even when the morning sun starts to sting, a cool breeze purls among the boulders here. One gallery of rock paintings displays fishes in the X-ray style, depicting internal structures in red lines on soft yellows. Powerful spirits glare from the rock. One is Namarrgon, the Lightning Man; the stone axes on his head and elbows split clouds and trees.

Bark painting charged with secret meaning still flourishes in Arnhem Land. I met artist David Malangi there, near Ramingining, and watched him decorate the smootheddown bole of a stringybark tree, a traditional emblem of mourning. He had painted a black band near each end, laid earth-red tones between them, and outlined the sinuous contours of king brown snakes in rich yellow. He added white cross-hatching with perfect precision. Finally my young charter pilot asked, with deference, "Would you teach a whitefellow to paint?" The artist smiled: "Can you get some leave?" It would take four or five days, he said, to learn basic techniques. Mastery, of course, requires years, and more than time.

In the region Australians call the "empty north" aviation links scattered communities. Cape York has a flying postman, the diocese of Carpentaria a flying bishop, Darwin a flying piano tuner. The northwest has a flying veterinarian whose career has been summed up as "All Creatures Far and Wide." He is David Bradley, working out of Kununurra. In 1986 he tested about 400,000 cattle for tuberculosis, over as many square miles. "This is probably the best cattle-breeding country in the world," he told me; "good river systems, and one of the most secure rainfall areas. The Wet's due any day now." Grasses flourish in the Wet, but cattle must survive by browsing scrub in the dry months. "Often cows with unweaned calves are very poor after the Dry. It's very hard country, very unforgiving."

Dun and scruffy, blotched with cloud shadows and eroded into jigsaw puzzle oddments, the land sprawled beneath David's Mooney 201 when we took off one sweltering afternoon for the Moolooloo Outstation on the famous Victoria River Downs property. Once more than 12,000 square miles, the "Big Run" now carried 100,000 head on 4,772 square miles—roughly, one beast to 30 acres.

Ian Rush was at the airstrip, a lean man with a sleek helmet of dark hair and a habit of talking with his lips closed. In the saddle at age 4, Ian was a jackaroo at 16, learning a stockman's skills to become a station manager. Francine Rush, fair-skinned and unweathered, was a Canberra girl. "She'd never done stock work before she came here in 1984," Ian said; "now she's the best stockman I've got."

Their home had the functional elegance of the outback: the one-story house with metal roof and wide veranda; stockmen's quarters nearby; a gum tree; a windmill pumping water from a bore. We sat under the tree with icy beers while the hot wind raised dust into a vivid sunset. Ian talked shop with David, then told me how he had hired a bloke who needed a job desperately. He swore he could ride—then landed in the saddle with his face to the horse's rump.

Before dawn we had eaten breakfast. At the workplace seven stockmen joined Ian and David and prodded the cattle, a few at a time, into a narrow chute marked "Walk Through Cattle Crush." Zebu-Shorthorn crossbreds, these animals showed every variation of appearance and temperament. As each went by, it received a TB shot and a vaccine against botulism. Calves bawled like 776 mangled trombones; iron gates clanged in a penitentiary frenzy.

Ian shouted destinies: "Breeder! Breeder! Meatworks! Weaner! Meatworks coming up next!" A cow got her head snagged between the rails of the crush; her horns had to be sawed off while she screamed in bovine soprano.

As the sun slid upward, and the heat with it, swirling dust glowed golden in backlight—romantic, but not for breathing. Dun . . . blaze face . . . brindle. "One more crush and that's about it." By 9 a.m. some 800 head had been injected, sorted, and earmarked. David estimated that preventive medicine had given the station 300 weaners that would have been lost otherwise—but they faced rugged foraging. There isn't enough water in the Victoria River in late November to irrigate pasture for weanlings. "It's such bloody hard country. . . ."

But people on cattle or sheep stations always tell you, "It's the real Australia." □

FOLLOWING PAGES: At home on the range in Western Australia, helicopters muster cattle on stations of the storied Kimberley region. Pioneer drovers "overlanded" stock here in historic outback crossings.

OLIVER STREWE / WILDLIGHT; PHOTO INDEX / ROGER GARWOOD (BELOW)

Station hands in the Kimberley wrestle with dust and haze to brand cattle early in the day—before tropical heat and humidity descend. On an Aboriginal reserve in central Australia, a stockman ties his mount after roundup (left). Their knowledge of the land and savvy with animals made Aboriginal stockmen indispensable; they tackled the job— one of the few open to them—with skill and enthusiasm.

Thunderhead gathers above Gwalia, north of Kalgoorlie. Gold lured fortune seekers to

Western Australia:
A Third of the Continent

this sere land in a giant state fringed by northern tropics and idyllic southern verdure.

Australia struggled for many years, historian Geoffrey Blainey has said, against its unofficial ruler: the tyranny of distance. One state in particular still spars with this tyrant, and that's Western Australia. A third of the continent in area, at 975,920 square miles it's larger than Alaska, Texas, and Arizona put together. It includes horizon-wide expanses that fit Mark Twain's line about "a climate which nothing can stand except a few of the hardier kinds of rocks." It also includes reaches of idyllic country, and I sampled both extremes.

Up north at Kununurra, in the Kimberley region, I saw something of the Ord River Irrigation Area, one of the nation's notable engineering schemes. Before the first of two dams was completed in 1963, the Ord would shrink to water holes in the Dry. In the Wet it might run seven million gallons a second. Now Lake Argyle can store 5.7 million acre-feet of water, but one crop after another has failed, often for economic reasons. Tropical fruits flourish here; distant cities offer good markets but daunting transportation costs. The old tyranny. I heard great things about (Continued on page 104)

OLIVER STREWE / WILDLIGHT; ©PETER WALTON / AUSCHROMES (ABOVE)

Loaded with water, spares, and provisions, a four-wheel-drive wagon shoots by the spinifex along the Gunbarrel Highway. Built in the 1950s, the road cuts through 862 desert miles in Western Australia, South Australia, and the Northern Territory; stretches run die-straight for 30 miles. Spiny-leaved spinifex grass (opposite) exudes a sticky gum gathered by Aborigines for hafting axheads and spearheads; the seeds, ground into flour, provided food.

High rises and a century-old fig tree (opposite) shade the Cloisters, built in 1858 as a school for boys. Perth got its nickname "City of Light" when it illumined itself as a landmark for astronaut John Glenn. Skyline (above) peaks at the building named for tycoon Alan Bond, whose victorious yacht Australia II *brought the America's Cup to Perth in 1983. At right, contenders* Kookaburra III *(in foreground) and* Steak and Kidney *compete to defend the cup in 1987.*

a new cashew project—"Australia will take over the world supply!"—and heard much later that it hadn't worked out as planned.

A wetlands zone, however, marks a success, as a cruise boat captain said. "These reedbeds and trees weren't here 25 years ago—just overgrazed banks crumbling away." Warblers were singing in the reeds beyond tiny white water lilies; long-toed jacana birds stalked about on the lily pads; an egret's bill closed on a silvery little fish. Cattle had overtaxed the country, but wildlife was returning.

In the Kimberleys, it's said, people drink hot beer right off the truck. I can see why. One humid day at 43°C—109°F—and rising, a bearded local told me, "If you can manage 43 you can manage 48, luv." The temperature at the airport reached 53°C, which is 127°F. I managed. I retreated to my air-conditioned motel. The room's mini-fridge supplied ice, and two nations were supplying books.

When I first traveled Down Under, in the 1960s, I had run out of current regional reading. Now I could hardly keep up with new titles. Some had won international honors: Britain's Booker Prize for fiction went to New Zealand's Keri Hulme in 1985 for *The Bone People*, to Australia's Peter Carey in 1988 for *Oscar and Lucinda*. Some authors challenged the cult of the he-man, or the white man; some flayed the government; some explored history. In the Kimberleys I read Mary Durack's pioneer saga, *Kings in Grass Castles*. Men of her family had taken four mobs of cattle overland from Queensland to the Ord in the 1880s, and built an empire. Now, however, Lake Argyle covered the site of her childhood home and an open-pit mine nearby had become the world's largest producer of rough diamonds, 30 million carats a year, most of them industrial grade.

I hoped to visit the mine, but an industrial dispute closed it for a time. I settled for Broome, glamour town of the northwest coast, known for a superb white beach, a new posh resort, and a gaudy past in the pearl trade.

Essentially, says one of its specialists, "Broome is pearling." Today it's cultured pearling. Marine biologist Bill Reed and his partners run pearl farms where skilled technicians inject young oysters with a bit of mussel shell. Given time, the oyster may cover the irritant with glowing nacre—mother-of-pearl. "The best Broome pearl is the best in the world," Bill said flatly. "The high yearly variation in water temperature—14 degrees—gives the quality. The characteristic Broome color is this lustrous silver white." He held up a dazzling example. His partner Alan Linney, a goldsmith, often sets the pearls with Argyle diamonds. He showed me gems of delicate pink, and others ranging from brown to palest yellow, marketed as "cognac" or "champagne." At the time, some very high-powered Westralian business deals were looking wobbly. Would this hurt Alan and Bill? "Oh," said Bill cheerfully, "when the executives and financiers aren't buying, lawyers and accountants become our clients."

Once, when the national economy was wavering, I discussed its troubles with an Aussie diplomat. "No worries," he said; "somebody will go out and dig up something." That's economic history for you, in a country that likes the nickname Oz. Mining booms have recurred ever since settlers in South Australia struck copper in the 1840s. In the northwest, the rust-colored land of the Pilbara region holds ore deposits estimated at 37,000 million metric tons, one of the richest iron reserves on earth. Other treasures probably await discovery.

I ran into an exploration geologist, a soft-spoken young expert named Peter Graham, who scouts this terrain. Gold was still going strong, he said; silver was "lying around waiting for the price to go up." At the moment, nickel was dead. I had heard of one boom that ended with the definition of a nickel mine as a hole in the ground owned by a liar. Platinum would be "significant," Peter said, and rare earths were "trendy." Peter liked the idea of settling in New Zealand someday, in the South Island. He was the only Aussie I met with this ambition. But he works in country like that near Marble Bar, notorious as one of the hottest areas in Australia. In the summer of 1923–24 Marble Bar had recorded 100°F for 160 days running.

Aside from mineral wealth the region has yielded a trove of earth history. Southeast of Port Hedland, near Marble Bar, lie 3,500-million-year-old fossils—the oldest known life-forms. To the southwest geologists have found tiny grains of zircon formed 4,300 million years ago. And so long as a few elders remember the traditional learning of their youth, human prehistory has not yet ended.

"Shine on, Perth!" runs the slogan. I'm sure it will. Of all the capitals in the sunburnt country, Perth boasts the most clear days in a year. Sunshine spills through the clear air onto the skyline hills, the sprawling low-rise suburbs and the soaring high-rise center. "Only 25 years ago this was essentially a two-story city," said a friend one night at a floating restaurant in the Swan River estuary. Boom times haven't canceled Perth's pride in its welcome-stranger atmosphere. I met an insurance man from London who had come to Perth with his wife, starting a worldwide search for an ideal spot to settle down, and gone no farther. "We came, we saw, it conquered," he explained.

"It's the most pleasant place to live, really laid-back," according to Cal (the Black Pearl) Bruton, a native of New York City, a naturalized Aussie, and general manager of a pro basketball team, the Perth Wildcats. This sport, a mania of mine, is becoming one of the most popular in Oz, a nation that often defines itself in sport and its heroes. The level of play is improving here, said Cal. His team's style is "Run—stun—have a lot of fun," and the slogan, naturally, "The West against the Rest."

Westralians have always been wary of "t'othersiders," residents of the dim distance known as E.S. or Eastern States. In the Great Depression they voted two to one to secede from the Commonwealth and become an independent state within the British Empire, but London squelched the plan. Actually, the state takes a national pattern to extremes: Perth holds 1,137,800 of its people, with a mere 442,000 left over. In many respects this means "a very centralized system," as Dr. Max Angus put it.

Dr. Angus is executive director of state schools, with an office in headquarters big enough to shelter a small town. "We're trying to decentralize," he told me, "to give local communities more of a say." At Christmas Creek, he said, on the fringe of the Great Sandy Desert, there's one school, with a shed for a town hall, a few houses, and an outlying population of 364. The community had gladly filled the shed for a meeting on school improvements.

Perthites live, they say, in the world's most isolated city. Here isolation isn't what it was. Faxed lab reports keep Dr. Byron Kakulas's research team in daily touch with specialists abroad, including those in my hometown of Durham, North Carolina. These groups study muscular dystrophy and related diseases. Dr. Kakulas has an omen of hope in the quokka, a small local wallaby. In 1960 he found that vitamin E could cure paralysis in quokkas; their damaged muscles regenerated completely—something previously thought impossible. "When we discover the exact cause, in biochemical terms, we may find a treatment for humans," he told me.

Another of the state's and nation's distinguished figures is Dame Mary Durack, whom I met one afternoon at tea. She has white hair and blue eyes and roundedness enough for the ideal grannie in a children's story, of which she has written several. She told me about one of her favorite projects, the Stockman's Hall of Fame and Outback Heritage Centre at Longreach, Queensland. That's her ancestors' country, "still *seething* with my relatives." She talked of R. M. Williams, a founding member of the Hall of Fame, who, as a penniless bush boy, made himself his first pair of shoes. Since then he has made a fortune with outback clothing and leather goods. "Ours is the democracy of the struggling majority, hoping for collective security—not the American democracy of abundance." I accepted more tea and cookies, feeling a bit guilty.

We discussed her state's abundance of good writers. Dame Mary had written a foreword for Colin Johnson's *Wild Cat Falling*, the first published novel by an author of Aboriginal blood. She urged me to read Tim Winton's fiction. "And have you read *My Place*, by Sally Morgan?" People were asking me that all over the country. This best-selling autobiography tells how a young woman learned of her part-Aboriginal ancestry and came to know her black kin.

Dame Mary grew up with a genuine affection for the Kimberley district and its people, including the Aborigines. Among them was "young Ernie" Bridge. His father was of Irish descent, a battler. A battler is somebody who's hard up but never gives up; he or she commands respect. Today, in his 50s, young Ernie's a man of mark as a singer of bush ballads and a member of the state parliament. He told me about droving trips when he would sing at night to soothe the cattle, hoping to head off a stampede. He rode one of the first helicopters that came out to help with the musters; one of his hit songs, about an airborne stockman, is "The Helicopter Ringer."

When I met him in a spacious office, he held three portfolios: minister for the northwest, for Aboriginal affairs, and for water resources. He stressed the importance of land tenure for Aboriginal people. Perth's water use worried him. "We're already drawing on groundwater," he said. He had his eye on Lake Argyle in the Kimberleys, with "195,000 times Perth's present consumption stored up there." Economists estimated forbidding costs for that supply; the lake was more than 1,400 miles away. A grin played over the minister's blunt features: "Economists—they're paid to tell you that whatever you want to do is impossible."

Like an unsound economist, I thought it impossible for Western Australia to live up to the nickname Wildflower State. Frank and Maureen Johnson corrected that with a swing through the southwest. He's a retired physician, she's in real estate, both are keen amateur botanists. They know the "wet eucalypt" forests—tuart, tingle trees, fine-grained jarrah and karri that seem impossibly tall after dry-country scrub. They also know the plants that fill understory and open country with color in spring. "Every year we find new flowers," Maureen told me, "even though we've lived here all our lives."

Early one rain-sprinkled November morning we headed south from Perth. By midday, at Bunbury, I had borrowed a warm jacket to check chill breezes off the Indian Ocean. Time and again, for four days, we stopped for wildflowers, all new to me. The state emblem, red-and-green kangaroo paw, seems meant for a child's crayons; a relative has bold yellow and black petals. I noted plants I wish I could grow: a *Leschenaultia* with delft blue flowers; pink *Pimelea*, Swan River myrtle, fragrant boronia; white clematis and spider orchids; golden *Hibbertia;* even a sharp-spined beauty called ouchbush and a small tree known as snottygobble.

Two delightful family visits brought national issues into perspective. Near the timber mill town of Pemberton, the Johnsons' son Murray showed me second-growth forest. "In 80 years of heavy logging," he said grimly, "the rainfall here has gone down by half." Gone with the trees were the leaves that returned water to the atmosphere. The second growth was full of tangles and silence, but in virgin groves of karri and jarrah unseen birds repeated their wild lyrics: chirps, trills, twitters—the sweetest I've ever heard.

Maureen's forebears were pioneers in the shire of Boyup Brook, lovely rolling country as good as any in the region. Her nephew Graham Moore runs 8,000 fine merinos on 4,942 acres at Denninup Vale. Here green paddocks surround a homestead where mellow antiques and elegant gardens suggest prosperity unalloyed. But Graham pointed out low ground tinged with the eerie gray-white of Lake Eyre. Salt. "No production off that at all," he said.

With trees cut down, no longer drawing moisture from the soil, the water table rises. In much of Australia, that brings salt toward the surface. Salt is already costing the nation nearly 500 million dollars a year and threatens its most productive agricultural zones.

"We're trying to reclaim these places with terraces and drains," Graham went on. He and his neighbors are planting salt-resistant blue gums, efficient living pumps, to lower the water level.

"Soil erosion and salinity—our biggest problem, and not something you can picket," said Graeme Campbell. He's a rangy, blue-eyed plainsman, survivor of an accident with faulty dynamite, federal representative for the largest voting division in the Western democratic world. That's almost the whole state minus the Perth metropolitan area. By 1988 it had 71,451 registered voters, from the tropical north to the blustery coast of the Great Australian Bight, a span of some 1,300 miles. Politicians need to get out and listen to the people, says Graeme. He manages with the help of a generous travel allowance and the certainty that "at least I won't get snowed in."

In his office at Kalgoorlie, under a huge map of his huge district, our conversation ranged, inevitably, far and wide. He spoke of the problems of setting telephone rates nationwide ("we have the best rate system for remote areas"), of the possibility of storing the world's radioactive waste ("we have the best technology and the most stable rocks").

That idea appeals to Doug Daws, a feisty character who was chairman of the Kalgoorlie Development Corporation when I met him. "What do you do with an old gold town?" he asked dramatically. Kalgoorlie flourished after prospectors found Australia's richest reef here in 1893, waned whenever world gold prices sank. Doug lost his job "like everybody else" when the mines closed in 1976, "a bit of a bloody blow." He was sick of an economy "doing this like a porpoise"—one hand traced ups and downs in the air. He thought hazardous-waste disposal a natural. "We're used to it. Mining means daily doses of cyanide and caustic soda and explosives."

Tourists who like ghost towns can find the relics nearby, the live reality here. Kalgoorlie was in one of its up phases, quivering as drills gnawed at the rock under it. New equipment was reclaiming gold from spoil heaps. And here I met a couple of Aussie battlers devoted to a very different kind of reclamation.

Des Arrow and Gail Allison, of the state's Alcohol and Drug Authority, defy burnout. He's a slight, cordial man whose parents came from Burma; she's a quiet, sturdy woman, and some of her forebears were Aboriginal. With the help of other agencies, they run a program that serves meals to people—black and white—who might not eat otherwise. In winter they take hot breakfasts to fringe dwellers who sleep among the slag heaps and under the pipeline that brings water pumped 351 miles from Perth. They counsel victims of less blatant stress. Women don't mind asking for help, says Des; too often, Aussie myths of manhood lead men to stifle their emotions.

Gail and Des serve an area from Esperance, 200 miles south, to Wiluna, 300 miles north. Gail told me how an emu farming project at Wiluna was struggling to meet demand; it needed a hatchery, she said. Emu leather is an haute couture item. Emu eggs, cut in low relief, are like cameos with a color range from pallor to a deep, matte blue green. Gail brought out one, carved by her brother, that filled my gingerly cupped hands with the most astonishing, fragile work of art I saw Down Under.

Why, I muttered before sunrise, am I leaving Kalgoorlie? But I love trains, and I had a ticket for the eastbound Trans-Australian, departing at 6:30 a.m. Smoke from a distant smelter stood vertical on the brightening sky when we pulled out past dusty spoil heaps, a last headframe over a mine shaft, a scatter of beer cans. The landscape faded to brindle, stunted gray stuff in yellow grass. I remembered what a geologist had said of this terrain, at half speed for emphasis: "It isn't going to be settled. It just . . . isn't . . . going . . . to . . . be."

Spinifex and mallee scrub flashed by, salmon gums and she-oak. What was growing there 30,000 years ago, in the cold rainy centuries? Were families roaming there, hunting, trading ornaments?

All morning the land lost relief until we entered the Nullarbor Plain, the flattest expanse of the flattest continent, roughly 75,000 square miles of limestone. "No-tree" Plain in amateur Latin, it holds a scattering of stunted growth, a few human outposts. It offers a journey like no other, on a paralyzed ocean of stone with daylight and darkness for its only tides.

Often described as dreary, the emptiness fascinated me for the simple reason that here any feature seems remarkable. Why are three mature trees growing knee-high over there? Why is a single willy-willy twisting its funnel of dust off to the south? Why is a lone kangaroo hopping along in the heat? Why is the corpse of a newish sedan resting there without its wheels?

By 5:30 p.m. shadows were thickening and lengthening until a boulder about the size of a footstool looked as imposing as Uluru. We had entered South Australia, at a border unmarked by anything natural. After nightfall we stopped briefly at Cook, where volunteers sell souvenirs to help support the hospital. I bought envelopes that reproduce a hand-lettered local sign, famous for good Aussie bluntness: "Our hospital needs your help—get sick." A string of streetlights was all we could see of the tiny settlement. Then, and long into the night, the rest of the universe was dark under its glitter of constellations, unsurpassable stars. □

Wet forest of karri trees in Porongurup National Park contrasts with arid plains over most of the state. Harvested for structural timber and hardwood flooring, these eucalypts reach to more than 250 feet. Kingias (opposite upper) are also known as grass trees and drumheads—for obvious reasons. Wildflowers grace the southwest, including the brilliant state flower, the kangaroo paw, and the banksia, whose nectar and pollen feed a tiny honey possum.

AUSTRALIAN PICTURE LIBRARY / JOHN CARNEMOLLA;   ROBIN SMITH (LEFT)

FREDY MERCAY / AUSTRALASIAN NATURE TRANSPARENCIES

I. R. McCANN / AUSTRALASIAN NATURE TRANSPARENCIES

Fair go, spinner! *The "spinner" at a Perth casino swings the "kip," flinging up two coins for another toss in the popular Aussie gamble, Two Up. Spinners become winners or losers with double heads or tails. East of Perth the gold-mining town of Kalgoorlie attracts tourists with handsome period pieces like the Old Australia Hotel (above) and a lingering notoriety for gambling and ladies of easy virtue. Moralists have condemned Two Up, but the game goes on. "Our country," wrote the Australian author Frank Hardy, "was pioneered in the spirit of a gambler's throw."*

FOLLOWING PAGES: Dunes roll seaward along the Nullarbor Plain on the south coast of Western Australia. A resident once remarked, "When it rains here, it's a mistake."

Searching for an inland sea in 1845, Charles Sturt found instead stony wastes and

South Australia and Tasmania:
Two Legacies

"sand-ridges of a fiery red"—the Sturt Stony Desert of South Australia.

"Adelaide's where the dateline is," said one official happily. The city was making news with Formula One racing cars screaming through the streets in the Australian Grand Prix, sponsored by Foster's beer. The 82-lap finale came on Sunday. On Sunday, in the old "city of churches," alias Wowser Capital of the Wowser State. A wowser is a killjoy, a bigoted sourpuss; wowserism has been defined as the English Nonconformist conscience running wild in Oz like prickly pear. In fact, dissenting Protestants settled South Australia in 1836 to escape England's oppressive laws. Here Christians would enjoy freedom of conscience, prosperity, and good learning. Their children should not grow up "poor, ignorant, and democratical," warned a leader, like the "white savages of Kentucky."

South Australia's traditions have focused on large matters as well as small. Time and again she has set an example in enlightened governance for her neighbors. In the 1890s she gave women the vote, provided for progressive taxation and free schools, and reformed her labor laws. Since the 1960s she has pioneered in protecting consumers, securing Aboriginal land rights, *(Continued on page 126)*

BILL BACHMAN;   PHOTO INDEX / RICHARD WOLDENDORP (OPPOSITE)

DAVE WATTS / AUSTRALASIAN NATURE TRANSPARENCIES

Camel, wombat, and kangaroo at any unexpected moment can vie for the right-of-way on the Eyre Highway. Views of wildlife enliven the trip, but travelers often find the stocky wombat a casualty on the thousand-mile drive across the arid Nullarbor Plain, an ancient seabed that edges the Great Australian Bight (opposite). In 1841 Edward Eyre explored it, drinking dew to survive; he found it "the most wretched . . . country imaginable."

FOLLOWING PAGES: River red gums and rock walls of changing hue star at Wilpena Pound, a natural amphitheater in the Flinders Ranges.

AUSTRALIAN PICTURE LIBRARY / JOHN CARNEMOLLA

ROBIN SMITH; © JEAN-PAUL FERRERO / AUSCAPE (RIGHT)

Barossa Valley vineyards, teeming with fruit at harvesttime,
have their roots in Old World traditions. German settlers
came to this gentle hill country in the 1840s, acquired
the vintner's art, and in time produced wines that won wide
acclaim. At the biennial Vintage Festival residents kick off
their shoes in a grape-stomping, wine-bibbing celebration of
the German heritage. Another emigrant that took root,
Echium plantagineum *(opposite) riots beneath red gums.*
The smothering weed bears two common names: Paterson's
curse, after the man who inadvertently spread it, and
Salvation Jane, livestock sustenance during long droughts.

"Putting down fruit," volunteers preserve locally grown Golden Queen peaches at Binglewingle, a historic homestead near Berri in South Australia. Croplands flourished here with Murray River irrigation; but salts concentrate in the soil, endangering vineyards and groves of citrus and stone fruits.

Cooked by a hundred-degree afternoon, a traveler floats luxuriously in a brimming stock tank on the Nullarbor. To fill the tank, windmills draw water from pools beneath the limestone plain.

and assuring equal opportunity for all. And she has scrapped a host of blue laws associated with the wowser spirit. "Adelaide may seem sedate," one resident confided, "but it's a real little sin-bin."

With more than half a million saints and sinners, the city spreads beyond its old avenues and bayshore into the lovely, perilous Adelaide Hills. Bushfires, such as those that ravaged the hills on Ash Wednesday of 1983, have seared some of the saddest dates into local memory. Happier anniversaries come from the city's arts festival, a biennial revel since 1960. "Oh, you lucky Adelaide people," satirist Barry Humphries said then, "you can get all that culture out of your system in two weeks and not have to think about it again for another two years." Not quite. Today the state devotes more than 30 million dollars a year to spreading culture through its system, to lonely outposts as far as Cook and Ceduna and the old camel-train stop en route to Alice Springs known as "Oodna-bloody-datta."

I made a point of revisiting the state's distinguished art gallery. Here 19th-century oils captured unspoiled forests and sunny plains as explorers saw them. Acrylics from the past 20 years portrayed sites of the central desert as Aboriginal artists know them; brilliant patterns of dots evoke the spotty tufts of vegetation and the sacred legends. A bark painting by David Malangi reminded me that from 1863 to 1911 the colony's unwieldy domain ran north all the way to the sea, encompassing the vastness of today's Northern Territory.

Although "nobly depressing rectitude" is a historian's phrase for South Australia's high-minded legacy, I met some lively inheritors and beneficiaries. Kym Bonython, scion of a public-spirited establishment family, spun fine yarns from his years as sheep farmer, jazz impresario, racing driver, and art dealer. Horst Salomon told me how he came in 1939 to escape Nazi persecution in Germany and has prospered as an entrepreneur.

Dame Roma Mitchell began her law career in 1934. "Some firms wouldn't brief a woman," she said, "but I never had problems with a lay client and the judges were quite good." A brisk, down-to-earth person, she was the first woman in Australia to sit as a judge on a state supreme court. She has chaired the nation's Human Rights Commission—finding the worst abuses in "fading little country towns." She's chancellor of the University of Adelaide. "Higher education for women was rare before World War II," she recalled. "Many women had nothing to talk about except babies and cooking and clothes, and the conversation of most girls was very dull."

"We've come a long way in one sense, removing legal discrimination, but we still have a long way to go," said John Moriarty, at the time director of the state's Office of Aboriginal Affairs. He belongs to the first group of Aboriginal university graduates, with degrees won in the 1960s. His experience of mission schools reflected official policy in years when certain children were chosen to benefit from white culture. "These expeditions came out to snatch kids who were a little paler than their mothers—who would run after the cars, screaming." I thought of the penal colony years, of English mothers screaming and weeping at waterside as the ships sailed.

"I tend to lead a dual life," John remarked. One part of his life is centered in his suburban home; the other lies across the continent in his traditional homeland. The suburb isolates the nuclear family on its small plot, he said; the ancient community gives a wide kindred in a spacious home. He told me about reunions on the clan estate by the Gulf of Carpentaria: "You live outside with the flicker of the campfire and the sounds of the bush and the laughter and all the things of the old days." He reminded me of the family reunions of my own childhood when he said, "Retelling the stories gives the old people a great deal of strength."

Friends of his, Peter and Margaret Lehmann, know the stories that people of the Barossa Valley have retold in German. Here settlers from Prussia found religious toleration; their Lutheran churches kept the language alive, and for many years they stood out as an exotic community, not least for their vineyards. Many regions— scattered from the Swan Valley and Margaret River in Western Australia to the Hunter Valley in New South Wales—produce splendid wines; the Barossa adds ethnic charm, stolid as sausage. Peter was away on the affairs of his prizewinning winery during my visit, but Margaret put the valley on parade as "viticultural paradise."

We followed winding roads through straw-gold slopes and tidy vineyards, to "very *Deutsch*" towns with steep-pitched roofs, Silesian style. Margaret pointed out massive trees by a small creek: "They're river red gums, and they're saying 'I own this land.'" We called at a stone barn converted to a winery by Joan and Howard Haese; he poured a fragrant white for us and identified furnishings as "genuine old pieces of family rubbish." We stopped on a sun-swept hill to sample Rocky O'Callaghan's Basket Press Shiraz—as Margaret said, "a great big round warm teddy bear of a wine." We inspected the Lehmanns' new stainless steel equipment, which she called "a PR man's nightmare—no atmosphere—and a winemaker's delight." Finally, after a long luncheon of suave food and beguiling vintages, I returned in a contented trance to Adelaide, an hour's drive south. I had to pack, to leave the driest state of the Commonwealth for its opposite: the wettest, greenest, smallest state—haunted, haunting Tasmania.

"They leave us off the map," Tasmanians say, and sometimes a map or logo does omit the heart-shaped island. "A lot of things pass us by," a young woman in Hobart told me wistfully. Much as Westralians speak of t'othersiders, Tasmanians speak darkly of mainlanders, a suspect mob. A bit larger than West Virginia, "Tassie" has about half a million people. More of them live outside the capital area than in it, and all of them, it often seems, are kin. "Marry a Tasmanian," a mainlander told me, "and you marry the whole bloody island." My hostess at Launceston, a vivid little woman called Billie Scott, introduced her husband as "Rod, who has more cousins than anybody else in Tasmania."

From the moment we splashed in through a springtime gale, I admired the Scotts' hilltop farmhouse, with its family antiques and paintings of forebears' sailing ships—and its blazing hearths. Around it, green lowlands spread like threadbare velvet to skyline mountains. Today the Scotts run 14,500 sheep and 1,000 Aberdeen Angus on 28,000 acres; the original property was granted in 1804 to James Hill, "the first free settler in northern Tasmania."

Pioneers like Hill got land for nothing and convicts for a labor force, felons shipped down from Sydney, a sullen lot and often dangerous. In his fine book *The Fatal Shore*, the noted Australian author Robert Hughes calls this Tasmanian project "a muddled and squalid affair." The newcomers fought the Aborigines and wiped out most of them—in Hughes's words, "the only true genocide in English colonial history." Tasmania often takes the contradictions of Australia to extremes. On the one hand, years of violence and dread. On the other, green valleys and dramatic mountains, idyllic homesteads, historic little cities.

I remembered Hobart from the 1960s as a muted town between somber Mount Wellington and the shimmering estuary of the Derwent. Church spires and Georgian dignity marked the center. Now, with startling new high-rise structures and 180,000 people, it's still a place where three ladies can appear at a party in identical floral-print dresses. Its past, dating from 1804, ranks with the casino and the temperate summers as an attraction for mainlanders.

One chilly morning I took a coach from Hobart to the Tasman Peninsula, to revisit the old penal complex there. "The animals you see dead on the roads are wombats, possums, and echidnas—and a few Tassie devils," announced the driver. An odd mob, even in life. This possum's a handsome creature with glossy dark fur, but the wombat's a podgy, lumbering brute from a James Thurber drawing. The echidna, or spiny anteater, is a spike-coated egg layer. The devil is a small marsupial carnivore like Satan's idea of a guinea pig: a stubby, quarrelsome imp with a strong stench and a powerful bite, an unofficial state mascot. The shop at the Port Arthur Historic Site sells small vials labeled "Genuine Tasmanian Devil Dung" along with others marked "Convict Sweat."

Guarded by deep-shadowed forest, the site opens into sweeps of green hillside, English trees, ruins of rose brick. From 1830 to 1877, some 12,700 sentences were endured here; it held about one in six of the 73,500 prisoners sent to the island. Although planned as "an abode of misery" and dedicated to constant toil, although preserved as Australia's shrine of convict suffering, it was not the most cruel of prisons. One claimant to that title is Macquarie Harbour, on the west coast, founded as a "Place of Ultra Banishment."

"Only the worst convicts were sent here," say the guides at

Strahan, now a harborside home to 500 residents. Here, from 1822 to 1834, felons and guards were alone between unmapped ranges and ferocious sea. In that time, writes Robert Hughes, this was "the worst spot in the English-speaking world." Today it's an entry to some of Australia's finest wilderness, the Franklin and lower Gordon River Valleys, saved by public opinion after a campaign that divided friends and families on the mainland as on the island.

Tasmania's unique resource is water, usually managed by the state's Hydro Electric Commission. By the 1970s the HEC had dammed all the other wild rivers and planned to turn these two into a chain of lakes. Given to sudden floods, the Franklin hurls its rapids through narrow chasms in remote forest; for miles it's a river of no return; but its admirers sent in a raft party to record its marvels for color television. "We brought it into living rooms all over Australia," conservationist Bob Brown told me, "and the river spoke to the people for itself." Many concluded that the river was a national treasure, not just an asset for Tasmanian engineers and industry. By precedent and constitutional provisions, such matters had always been left to the states. Tasmania's premier spoke of secession if Canberra intervened; but the Labor Party promised to oppose the dams, and won a nationwide election in March 1983. The rivers still run free, unhindered, untainted.

"What was pivotal," Bob Brown explained, "was the fact that Australia had signed the U.N.'s World Heritage agreement in 1974. The High Court of Australia ruled that the Commonwealth's obligation to carry out a treaty must override states' rights in this case." To this day, World Heritage listing is crucial—and highly controversial—in battles over Australian wilderness.

I had unforgettable glimpses of the Tasmanian prize in a river cruise on the lower Gordon. Rain forest asserted itself in myrtle, with its bronze-tinged leaves; leatherwood; spirals of screw pine; tall celery top and Huon pines; white veils of springtime blossom at the water's edge. "It was very lively up here during the '83 blockade," the captain remembered, "like Sydney Harbour on a Sunday morning." Protestors had blocked the river with rubber rafts; 1,272 people had been arrested. Now a passenger was murmuring, "It's so serene. . . ."

Of all the places for serenity, I thought, this zone of convict torment. Of all the places for volunteers to get themselves arrested. By official records for just four years, precisely 33,723 strokes with a nine-tailed, triple-ply whip were cut into the backs of convicts. One survivor recalled how a man would be sent back to his toil after 100 lashes, "his back like Bullock's Liver and most likely his shoes full of Blood." Now the years of horror had become an incident in the wilderness, the wilderness a landmark for a nation. ☐

Shrine of convict suffering, the Penitentiary metes out
grim memories of England's dreaded prison, Port Arthur.
Now a historic reserve, the infamous complex on Tasmania's
southeastern coast held more than 12,000 inmates between 1830
and 1877. Theft of a handkerchief in England could bring a
sentence of transportation. In Australia a law broken by a
banished felon might land the miscreant in Port Arthur, often
shackled in irons. Incorrigibles were hobbled with heavy fetters,
flogged, and starved. Noted one Port Arthur observer: "Around
every stone must cling the ghost of a human agony, the
bitter and undying memory of floggings and an echo of the
last defiant curse of the hanged."

Luxuriant wilderness of eucalyptus, heath, and a beech shrub called tanglefoot surrounds Lake Dove in Cradle Mountain-Lake St. Clair National Park, whose namesake peak dominates the skyline. Horizontal scrub tangles the feet of bushwalkers in a wet forest of Southwest National Park (above). Glaciation ground southwest Tasmania into a jumble of dramatic beauty unmatched in Australia.

Young Tasmanian devils huddle in a den. Extinct on the mainland, the scavengers abound here, Tasmania's unofficial mascot despite a devilish reputation.

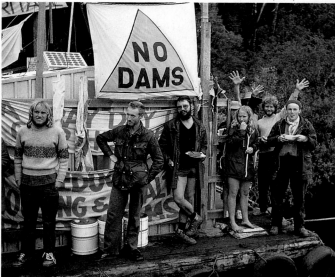

Tasmania's lower Gordon River flows untamed, a victory for conservationists who fought plans to dam the stream and its tributary, the Franklin. Protest leader Dr. Bob Brown (top) later rallied support to halt logging near Cradle Mountain. Of the grandeur he defends, Brown says, "It is an environment for finding a more rewarding self than exists in the everyday world."

FOLLOWING PAGES: Bob Brown thrashes through white-water fury pouring from rocky flumes of the Franklin.

Well-trodden Croajingolong National Park harbors a diverse realm—seashore and

Victoria:
Some of Everything

rain forest, sea eagle and lyrebird, and creatures of the night such as possums and gliders.

"You want to live, you come." Tuyen, from Vietnam, gave this succinct reason for coming to Australia. Tu Phuong, from Cambodia, said, "My country's too populated, and they're killing each other." To him, Australia is "freedom, and food enough to eat." Leo, from Uruguay, missed the occasional roast armadillo; Suzana, from Yugoslavia, found Christmas strange without snow; Franklin, from the Philippines, missed riding his grandmother's water buffalo. With classmates from Macao and Cyprus and other homelands, these teenagers were in an English-as-second-language course at a Melbourne high school. I was impressed by their fluency—they coped easily with my southern-Yank accent.

Only once, and in Melbourne, did someone who had heard me assume that I was Australian. "Oh," said the woman in question when I had explained, "we have some of everything here." Noted for its varied terrain and ecosystems, Victoria has acquired an even richer variety of people.

When Australia began actively seeking immigrants after World War II, policy called for Britons by (Continued on page 144)

Legends of a Wild East still haunt Victoria. Homemade armor, stylized in paintings by Sir Sidney Nolan, identifies the outlaw hero Ned Kelly, master of bushcraft and bank robbery, hanged in 1880. Told of the hangman's appointed hour, the most famous of all bushrangers replied, "Such is life." A gold rush in the 1850s turned an Aboriginal campsite, Balla-arat, into a boomtown. Today a local venture called Sovereign Hill re-creates the historic community. At its Gold Museum antique scales hold raw nuggets—small ones. Townsfolk say proudly, "Ballarat's gold built Melbourne."

Ornate Flinders Street Station serves subway and railway commuters in the heart of Melbourne. The copper-domed landmark in the French Renaissance style, completed in 1910, also serves as a rendezvous: "Let's meet under the clocks." Variety marks the broad byways of this cosmopolitan city that can boast of "some of everything" in architectural as well as ethnic styles.

preference, northern Europeans if possible. The minister for immigration arranged lavish publicity for the arrival of displaced persons from the Baltic—blue-eyed blonds. Blonds and Britons didn't come in sufficient numbers, however. The government cast its appeal wider. Aliens from the Mediterranean countries faced suspicion and hostility at first. As a teacher said of her own parents, "They were petrified of Australians and the Australians were petrified of them."

In 1972 the government scrapped the "White Australia" policy that had excluded Asians since 1901. The new immigrants often faced a wider cultural gap than had the earlier arrivals. Usually the newcomers struggled with the language. They heard the hostile epithets that may greet strangers anywhere but get special pungency from Aussie bluntness. Still, the children I met seemed to like Australia, without illusions. Parents fretted about the possibility that the kids would grow up too laid-back, adopting the casual style of "she'll be right, mate—no worries."

Immigration policy was a hot topic, especially the admission of Asians; quite a few citizens denounced the government's ideal of multiculturalism. Yet never once, in discussions with "New Australians" and "old" ones all over the country, did I hear a remark like "The kids will never fit in" or "They'll be a mob of dole bludgers." (Dole bludger means welfare cheat—fighting words.) One thoughtful youth of Asian parentage told me that some Australian boys are racist: "They show it by calling names; not a lot of them, but some do." In the epithet wars at one Melbourne school, the Aussies were "skips," from a TV series about Skippy the Bush Kangaroo—an ironic touch, I thought, given this supremely urban setting.

Sprawling over more than two thousand square miles, Greater Melbourne holds nearly three million people, all officially suburbanites except the 3,592 in the central city. Not even counting those from the British Isles and New Zealand, about 20 percent were born overseas—the highest total in Australia. Jobs help explain this concentration; this is the most industrialized part of a highly industrialized state. (A classic cartoon shows an immigrant confronting a clerk who's saying "Farmhand." "I'm a brain surgeon!" cries the newcomer. "Sorry," says the clerk, "auto assembly.") The preference of immigrants for a community of their own also plays a part. "You can eat your way around the world without leaving Melbourne," a tourism official told me happily; unfortunately, I had to leave long before I finished Asia, Italy, and Greece.

Often called the largest Greek city outside the homeland, Melbourne has more than a third of the 300,000 Greek-Australians. "A majority own their own businesses," journalist Steve Hatzimanolis told me. "We're very proud to be Australians, and we love Australia but we're *not* Anglo-Saxons." He chuckled, recalling a soccer match against Scotland: "All the 'British' Australians were supporting Scotland and all of us were cheering for Australia."

More than 380,000 Italians have come out since World War II. "Every week there's a barbecue for the Madonna of some small village," said Lydia Grescini, summing up a suburban social calendar. She and her husband, Giovanni or John as friends please, had arrived in 1955 and started out with a photo shop. I was struck by an account she had written of Australians as she had first seen them, silent passengers on buses and trams: "I can understand their silence towards a newcomer, but I don't know if they are like that among themselves. . . . Do people here have so many worries that they carry a shield of silence around them all the time?"

Despite the stereotype of the outgoing Aussie—"Crocodile" Dundee saying "G'day" to strangers in Manhattan—taciturn reserve is a widespread attribute, especially in cities. In 1955 Melbourne's noted artist John Brack caught that quality in his famous study of commuters, "Five O'clock Collins Street": a few women and many men in somber business garb, with long impassive faces and thin lips pinched shut. I saw people who might have posed for it, but they no longer dominate the city panorama.

In the business district, by the "Venetian Gothic" splendor of a historic bank, I saw a stumpy, aged woman in the timeless black of a Mediterranean village. At a suburban park on a weekend afternoon, I saw an immigrant wedding party in lavish finery observing a new ritual: posing for pictures among the flower beds. At the zoo, families in the styles of Pakistan and the Near East passed families in pure Aussie casual. The butterfly house offered an unforgettable vignette. Here, in an immense room full of greenery, hundreds upon hundreds of gorgeous insects flutter about as visitors pass among them. Some wear the golden orange of Kimberley sandstone; others flash scarlet or blue or green like the flares of color in a fire opal from Lightning Ridge. I noticed a burly, tattooed, sunburned man who would be the ideal ocker (the Aussie version of Joe Six-pack) for a beer commercial, the tough bloke in the blue singlet, chauvinist in every sense of the word. This specimen was crouching motionless, his massive right hand held out; and he was staring, absolutely rapt, at the dainty orange lacewing perched on the tip of his forefinger.

Along with such unpredictable attractions, Melbourne has its festivals and horse races; Aussie Rules football, a fluid, high-leaping game somewhat like rugby; and the splendid complex called the Victorian Arts Centre. Inevitably, the Centre invites comparison with the Sydney Opera House; the rivalry between these cities is a hoary national joke. A staff spokesman complimented the Opera House for its beautiful exterior, but said, "I don't think the interior has the same sense of detail as ours."

"Melbourne has more 19th-century buildings than any city except Leningrad," says one of its partisans. Many streets evoke imperial elegance. Plane trees reminded me of Paris, and the old Treasury and state Parliament buildings, finely sited on a hilltop among lavish gardens, suggest London with palm trees.

"A century ago," said legislator Mark Birrell at Parliament House, "you had the cathedral and theaters around here—and tents and dust. That tells you how quick the pace of development was. The House shows you how wealthy the colony was." With rich gilding—and electric fans as a minor incongruity—the legislative chambers had a grace and lightness I hadn't expected.

Mark is a member of the Liberal Party, which he described as right wing. It is a party with deep roots in Victoria. "We support free enterprise and equality of opportunity," he declared. Mark was eloquent on the role of the states, especially his own. "We wouldn't have a nation if we didn't have states. For a continent the size of Australia it's beyond belief that you could have a single government." If you believe in democracy, he maintained, you disperse power in a federal system.

"Ballarat's gold built Melbourne," says Peter Tobin. He's a rangy, dark-haired son of that historic town. Peter and his colleague Doug Sarah are directors of Sovereign Hill, an admirable re-creation of the gold rush center, and they talked of those days as we drove out from Melbourne—a scenic 90-minute run today, a grueling trek upland for bullock carts.

Only a few weeks after Victoria became a separate colony on July 1, 1851, fossickers stumbled onto gold. In no time prospectors were swarming over the inland. "At Golden Point," said Peter, "you could pull up a clump of grass and shake the dirt off and gold would fall out. It aroused a keen interest in gardening." As we toured Ballarat, he and Doug sketched its story: 1851—virgin bush; 1852—lunar landscape; 1861—city of 100 hotels on one street alone. Its gold production has been estimated at 630 metric tons, or 20,600,000 troy ounces. Men rushed in from Melbourne, from the other colonies, from New Zealand, from Europe. Americans arrived; many were forty-niners from California, which symbolized anarchy to colonial officials, just as Ireland symbolized rebellion.

None of the officials believed in democracy. A noted historian has called the first goldfields commissioner "a treacherous, barbaric thug." Many of the goldfields police were ex-convicts—in Peter Tobin's words, "the sweepings of the gutter." Law enforcement often amounted to a shakedown racket. Otherwise, crime was slight. The diggers created a social democracy of their own, and they wanted political rights. In November 1854 the Ballarat Reform League, 10,000 diggers strong, called for manhood suffrage and fair representation in the legislature as well as an end to abuses. It challenged Queen Victoria's royal prerogative by declaring that "the people are the only legitimate source of all political power."

At Ballarat's fascinating Gold Museum, I saw the most famous symbol of their cause: a huge blue flag, with five white stars on crossed white bands. The most determined diggers gathered round it on November 30 while their leader proclaimed: "We swear by the Southern Cross to stand truly by each other, and fight to defend our rights and liberties." A unique oath, to a flag that wasn't Britain's. A line in a diggers' poster caught my eye: "Who so base as be a slave?" Perhaps it had inspired an American who joined in. He was known locally as a lemonade vendor; he was tall, powerful, and black. His name was John Joseph.

The rebels built a crude bark-slab stockade on a gold site called Eureka. There, at daybreak on Sunday, December 3, they were crushed by a surprise attack of infantry, cavalry, and mounted police. They "fought hard and died harder," as a historian says. Officially, 5 soldiers and 30 miners died.

Charged with high treason, 13 of the rebels were tried in Melbourne. The first was John Joseph. A jury promptly acquitted him. Even though the Crown challenged any prospective juror of Irish origin, all 13 prisoners went free. Democratic reforms followed in short order, as public opinion carried the day.

"Eureka achieved all the things we take for granted," said Peter as we visited the grassy little park where the stockade had stood; "things like the citizens' vote, pay for legislators. But when we planned our 125th anniversary celebration, the Prime Minister wouldn't attend, and the minister of defense refused to let a military band take part, because it was 'too political.'"

"Eureka's an embarrassing subject," according to state historian Bernard Barrett. "People discuss sex openly, but Eureka causes ambivalence because it involves law and order." Of course a good citizen favors law and order. Still, as a prominent lawyer has said, many Australians "share a cantankerous and skeptical distrust of authority in all its forms." A park ranger told me that people who respect a "Road Closed" sign will remove a portable road barrier: "They just want to show us they won't be bossed."

If this defiant spirit has a single national hero, it's Ned Kelly, who was born about the time of Eureka, lived in northeast Victoria as the last of the great bushrangers, or wilderness outlaws, and was hanged in Melbourne in 1880 for the murder of a policeman. Son of an Irish convict from Tasmania, he denounced the "tyrannism of the English yoke" and scorned one hapless official as "a poodle dog half clipped in the lion fashion." Irish grievances and pride have been significant strains in Australia since 1788, and Ned Kelly's courage is still a byword. Nothing in sardonic Australian wit has bettered his comment on his own execution: "Such is life."

Braving the odds is still a national specialty, but the form has changed. "I threw security to the winds and, with boyish enthusiasm, set out to tackle the impossible," Professor Graeme Clark told me in Melbourne. A lean, elegant man, *(Continued on page 152)*

*A family odyssey, from nightmare to dream come true:
Thien Nguyen relaxes with a turbaned fellow bus driver,
part of the immigrant stream that flows into Melbourne.
An air force officer and journalist in war-ravaged
South Vietnam, Nguyen and his family fled with the "boat
people." Asians, who make up the largest group of new
arrivals in Australia, often face a difficult adjustment.
Most persevere. Smiling Kim Nguyen (above) won
acceptance at school. For her parents, hard work realized a
shining dream, a single-family house on its own lot.*

Hoofs fly in the Melbourne Cup, a world-class horse race and the occasion for a transcontinental bash. As Mark Twain wrote, "Cup Day is supreme." Ladies' clothes are "without bounds. . . . The champagne flows . . . everybody bets." Aussie sports lure armies of spectators, not all in formal attire. The fan at right wears tassels of corks and beer-can rings, a jocular reminder of large thirsts—and large quenchings—in a parched land.

RENNIE ELLIS / SCOOPIX (ALL)

he gave up his medical practice in 1966 to develop the invention called the bionic ear (formally, a cochlear implant). "Everyone said it wouldn't work—that 22 electrodes couldn't do the fine processing of sound that's normally done by 20,000 fibers in the inner ear. I said, 'It's a gamble, but let's get on with the job and see.'" It's strange, he observed, that Australians seem willing to bet on anything except their own innovators. Finally, with funding from the U.S. and Australian governments, he and his team produced the device and the surgery that offer hope to perhaps one or two million people deafened by auditory nerve defects.

Smallest of the mainland states at 87,884 square miles, most densely populated and most intensively farmed, Victoria seldom reminded me of the "mobs of nothing" interior. It often looked inhabited. A southern area won the label of "Australia Felix—Fruitful Australia" for its fertility. True, sand plains in the northwest rank as "Little Desert," and miles of mallee scrub are empty enough to make a broken beer bottle an appealing hint of civilization. Parks and reserves protect coastal cliffs, forests and scrub, the massive old Victorian Alps and lesser ranges. Still, there're towns enough to suggest that humankind has established itself. Some of the most pungent depend on the Murray River, "Australia's Mississippi."

Once, say proud citizens, Echuca was the busiest inland port in Australia, a link in a huge system. The Murray, 1,600 miles long, has a tributary 100 miles longer: the Darling, draining the so-called Channel Country in Queensland. The Murrumbidgee, at 980 miles, provided a total 3,600 miles of water that steamboats could use for perhaps eight months of a decent year. Given the wild quirks of rainfall, the waters might run 20 miles wide or shrink to isolated puddles. Still, between 1850 and the turn of the century, the paddle steamers took wool and timber down to South Australia and brought civilized items back. (In 1870 an English traveler noted that "forty thousand sheep cannot be shorn without a piano. . . .")

In this century dams and locks and weirs have stabilized the Murray system, allowing irrigation. "This country wouldn't be worth two bob without water; it wouldn't feed a billy goat," said Don Oberin of Echuca as we drove westward to visit his dairy farm. "Out here it's flat all right; that little range there's a landmark and it's 145 feet high." The road ran straight for nearly 20 miles. "See the condo?" I didn't. It proved to be a mulga tree, all of ten feet high, with two magpie nests. We passed sheep fretting in the relentless sun, shoving their heads under one another's bellies for a spot of shade. Green replaced brown, abruptly: irrigated land.

"See that scungy water?" We crossed a drainage channel. "It goes back to the Murray." With it go silt and fertilizer and, often, salt. The salinity load in the lower river is a slow, intractable crisis. Don's farm has 300 Friesians on 646 acres, and he expected to pay $80 or $90 an acre for laser grading to assure the best possible flow and drainage of water. He was planting trees to lower the level of salty groundwater. Salinity costs Victoria alone at least 40 million dollars a year, and New South Wales, across the Murray, was spending millions more. "As far as the valley goes, the river's everything," said Don; "90 percent of our incomes depend on the Murray."

As the river town closest to Melbourne, Echuca draws a host of visitors. They inspect the historic wharf and waterside area, lately spiffed up. They can cross the "Xylophone," the old bridge with wooden crossbeams, to gamble: New South Wales allows the pokies (poker, or slot, machines) and Victoria doesn't. They can camp by the water, or rent a houseboat, or ride a paddle steamer. I took a run upriver on the *Pride of the Murray*, once a barge that could move 45 logs (or 200 tons) of river red gum. Skipper Max Carrington pointed to a fine specimen: "He needs a flood every few years to grow well. His roots go very deep, and he can store water a long time." Manipulated flow has broken the old flood-and-dry-up cycles, and I wondered how long those trees would say, "I own this land."

Along the surprisingly narrow stream, kids swung from the high western bank to drop from a rope with a glorious splash. Three youths were hurling mud blobs at one another; lots of children were swimming. Summer current dawdles along at two or three miles an hour, with eight or ten in the sharper bends.

"It's the best river in the world," the captain said stoutly. "You can swim in it, fish in it, and you can still drink it." But, he conceded, he can no longer get a big basketful of fish whenever he wants. "Now you're lucky to get one fish."

Sometime later I joined the side-wheeler *Coonawarra* for part of her bicentennial cruise from Mildura to Goolwa, S.A., reenacting the old trade voyage. For our send-off, the mayor of Mildura appeared in full regalia, his white lace jabot crisp over a black robe with gold braid; a clergyman who blessed the voyage wore white vestments—and thong sandals. Mildura fruits were brought on board. TV cameras whirred, houseboats trundled up to see us off, whistles sounded, paddles started their refrain of whirr-flip-*splash* in opaque brown water.

"We're typical Australians, we own our homes, and we're taking a holiday!" said an expansive passenger called Maisie, and we settled into leisure. The Murray meanders so twistily that river distances triple their highway counterparts; we watched the banks slide by in stands of native scrub or tangles of exotic willows. We chatted and drank beer. A chap from Tasmania told of recent bushfires on the island: "We know how Pompeii felt!" We sunbaked, or retreated to air-conditioned shade. Small events became major diversions, such as a black swan's taking flight and leading us downriver. We saw a stockman rescue a wether that had slipped off the steep bank and couldn't climb back under its weight of sodden fleece.

Where the banks ran red with Coonawarra clay, at the Mildara Winery, we took on a huge cask for the new museum down at Goolwa. Once a whump-whump-whump throbbed through the boat as Captain Leon Wagner eased her over a sandbar. Officials upriver had released extra water for her benefit. Luckily such vessels were designed, it's said, "to float on a wet sack or a dewy lawn."

At Wentworth, "town of two rivers," we swung through the swirling confluence into the Darling, a narrow green-gold stream, and accepted a ponderous bale of wool from Avoca Station: the first wool shipped downriver since 1908. The captain also took custody of a package from Mrs. Dorrie Cooper; she had baked one of her celebrated fruitcakes for the Prince and Princess of Wales, who would open the museum. Old loyalties run deep in country districts. I suspect she would make mincemeat of the chap upriver who called Their Royal Highnesses "a couple of freeloading Poms." Poms, or Pommies, are Brits; freeloaders are a very low form of life.

We moored for the night above Lock 8, where a kookaburra jeered when some of us went for a bushwalk. We rambled along to a drying billabong, a shallow mirror ringed with cracking clay. The sun went crimson behind the gum trees, one of the men recited the poem that begins "I love a sunburnt country," and we sang "Waltzing Matilda" in a muted, sociable way. The night before, passenger Keith Graetz had played the most poignant rendering of it I ever heard. He used a long gum leaf, which gives a resonant music when held taut at the lips of an expert.

"Advance Australia Fair" has been the official anthem since 1984, "God Save the Queen" is still played on suitable occasions, but the nonofficial song is always "Waltzing Matilda," with its bush-ballad lilt and defiant lyrics. I've heard it as raucous in a Darwin pub, or meditative, a piano solo on a high-country station. I saw it acted out in Mildura, where Bozo the Clown was celebrating the bicentenary with local children. He chose a child for each character in the story, including the jumbuck—the sheep that the swagman-hero steals. He underlined the wealth of the squatter, landholder and villain of the story: "Down came the squatter, mounted on his BMW. . . ." Before the last stanza, when the swagman drowns himself, Bozo warned, "Now here's where it all gets very sad." Afterward he intoned a long quavering *"Wooooooo"* in honor of the swagman's ghost. It reminded me of a river ballad in which a Murray steamer, trapped by drought, breaks out on a sudden flood and takes her captain upriver into the eerie distance of legend.

I had to leave the *Coonawarra* and the river at Lock 8, going ashore early in the morning among enormous plastic sacks of empty tinnies, or beer cans. Shipmates turned out for a farewell song and some chaffing about "Yank luggage." The more ribbing you can take, the better you'll like it Down Under.

You could explore Victoria's protected wild areas for a long time; they add up to more than 7 percent of the state. Around Halls Gap, in the Grampian Mountains, you're at risk of Grampian stiff neck. That's the crick you get staring up into gum trees. Wild koalas clamber about up there, looking more cuddlesome than they are, while grey roos hop about the camping area expecting bread crusts.

Park rangers worry about local beekeeping. European honeybees bash their way into native flowers adapted to other pollinators, and the battered blossoms may not set seed. Still, the white clusters of Christmas bush filled the air with spicy sweetness when I was there. I wouldn't have recognized ranger Denis Rose as part-Aborigine—his eyes are green as the Darling—but he told me how a new Living Heritage Centre will preserve ancient traditions. Explaining bush tucker to visitors, he didn't mention that koalas are perfectly edible.

"If only we had time," said regional forestry official Allan Holmes, "I could show you 20 or 30 places in East Gippsland, and at each one you would be struck by the special beauty of that forest. The rivers are among the last pristine streams on the mainland. Our forest reserves are the best in Australia. But there's still room for improvement." We had met at his headquarters in Orbost, a pleasant town with a wind-sock airstrip. Roiling black thunderheads were filling the sky by noon, and Allan's radio crackled out news of a fire up-country. "A lightning strike this early in the day— that's bad news. Here fire is the unpredictable element."

Fires set by Aboriginal fire sticks regulated the mainland landscape for perhaps 400 centuries. Frequent small-scale burning promoted new grass in open country, gave woodland the clear parklike quality that impressed white explorers, and minimized the risk of devastating wildfires. "We need more research on fire frequency and intensity," said Allan, "to get a more responsible view of what the hell's going on in the bush, a rigorous scientific data base."

He kept his radio open when we set out in his four-wheel-drive vehicle for one of those special places. The up-country crews had things in hand. "Gippsland people have the reputation of being a bit redneck," he remarked, "but they're incredibly diverse: a strong working class—not hard people really—and alternative-life-style types, keen conservationists." We wound into the hills, through mature forest. Mountain grey gum; messmate stringybark, with its rough yellow-brown trunk; shining gum, with its smooth-barked bole; manna gum, with leaves that glint like ice when backlit. We came to true rain forest, of the warm temperate type. Lianas draped dense veiling over green wilderness. Suddenly a lyrebird dashed across the track, head low, long tail feathers trailing, like a heroine of melodrama fleeing into a storm. "They show enormous fright when you surprise them," said Allan happily. "They rush off as if the world's about to end. But they're the cheekiest birds imaginable, and they can imitate anything they hear—even bulldozers."

Turning toward the coast, Allan scowled at a creek where black-berry—yet another exotic plague—was crowding out tree ferns. He talked about the bicentennial. "It's a minor note at Orbost, no big deal." But he wanted to show me the family-camping cabins on the beach at Cape Conran. "That's a bicentenary project. Nothing fancy, but energy-efficient designs. And all natural woods."

Christmas trees were glittering in Melbourne windows. Just at the peak of the shopping season a commuter-train strike disrupted the area, and a men's shop advertised "SALE—Catch Us With Our Pants Down." A strike of armored-van guards threatened branch banks with a cash shortage. A beer strike, mercifully, never materialized. None of the shops I entered had a canned-music barrage; street musicians serenaded the business district. I joined old friends to sing carols on Christmas Eve, and new friends for a sumptuous cold luncheon on Christmas Day. The English hot dinner is disappearing, at last. Melbourne's notorious weather shifted within hours from chilly drizzle to sunny brilliance, ideal for cricket.

Despite the holiday break, I met the minister for conservation, forests, and lands at the most popular national park in her domain, Wilsons Promontory. Joan Kirner and her husband, Ron, were staying at headquarters there. The Prom's a granite dagger stabbing the tricky waters of Bass Strait. From Mount Oberon, at 1,765 feet, sweaty hikers admire the coastal ranges, white beaches, grassland, stands of that fine tree the lillypilly. "In spring," said Joan, "the honey myrtles and tea trees are like thousands of moonbeams—the whole place just shimmers." We crossed flat terrain where emus paced the car. Yellow-and-black cockatoos cried *brrrrarrrk*, alert as sentinels. In late afternoon, grey roos bounced lithely away from us and wombats ignored us, waddling and grazing.

Joan (who later became deputy premier) talked of old abuses. "In the 1920s and '30s, the barely arable mallee country was cleared and worked until the land just started to resist. Rabbits took over the selections [small farms]." She outlined efforts to restore degraded land, to improve forest policies, to establish marine parks, and to extend parks in the Victorian Alps. She analyzed public opinion. "The strongest feeling for conservation is in the eastern suburbs of Melbourne, the swing seats of the state Parliament." In good fair-go style, she complimented a formidable opponent and told me I should meet him: Graeme Stoney, of the mountain cattlemen.

Graeme and his son Chris gallop over daredevil's terrain in *The Man from Snowy River* movies, filmed near their home at Mansfield. Graeme carried an Australian flag in the vanguard when the cattlemen, 300 strong, rode their stock horses into Melbourne in 1984, appealing for public support. They were battling to keep the high-country grazing leases their forebears had held for more than a century. They opposed the state government's plans for one great alpine park, and won one of those crucial swing seats in Parliament.

Today the Stoneys lead ski-touring parties or trail rides, depending on the season, and I joined them for a New Year's party. Tension ran high on the bus heading up-country: Aussie and Kiwi cricketers were playing the deciding game of the yearly test match series. A radio was turned up to loudest. "New Zealand is just one wicket away from winning . . . and Australia is reeling. . . . The match has ended in a draw! What a magnificent game of cricket!"

Bipartisan and happy, I watched as ridges grew steeper, pastures richer. Small bright rivers purled through gentle vistas. "Mansfield's a holiday town now," said Graeme when we met, but the Stoneys still took 300 Herefords up to the mountaintops in summer, down to the valley in winter, as the battle over the park plan went on. He complimented Minister Kirner while we climbed the Howqua Valley in his 4WD: "A very able lady, with the toughest portfolio." He outlined the cattlemen's views. "All responsible groups have been calling for conservation." The debate focused on the effects of grazing. Some said it was destroying native herbage. The cattlemen said it reduced the danger of shrub dominance, calamitous bushfires, and subsequent erosion. Graeme pointed out spreading clumps of blackberry. "There're no votes in killing blackberry in the Alps! The state has more land than it can take care of already."

We stopped briefly at Sheepyard Flats, where the Howqua River riffles along as good fly-fishing water: white foam, white blossoms, white-barked trees, white cloud puffs above green-gold hillsides. Then higher into the Victorian Alps, which reminded me of the Great Smokies at home. We passed a big resort. "You never hear criticism of a great swath cut through the bush for a skifield—the ski lobby's too strong." At 5,200 feet, we reached The Bluff, a dramatic scarp. Rounded summits rose dark on the skyline. Soon the trail riders clopped in, ready for a feast of steaks in the pioneer's hut that the stockmen still use. The horses grazed among snow gums, to rest before the last day's trek down the valley.

Rain disrupted that plan. Next morning it planged on everything metal and thrummed on the tents, but the clouds had given New Year's Eve an eerie radiance, thickening around the moon. We gathered around a well-guarded bonfire, chatting and singing, and nobody noticed the Stoneys jockeying the 4WDs into new positions. We collected tumblers of champagne as watches eked out the last seconds of the year.

At midnight headlights blared as one. The beams converged to show Graeme standing on the pitched roof of the hut, champagne in his left hand and the national flag held high in his right. His voice rang strong: "A bicentenary toast to Australia!" We drank it, and we sang "Waltzing Matilda," and for some of us there was shimmer around the firelight and the flag and the moon. □

*"Australia's Mississippi," the Murray River meanders through
thickets of willow and stands of red gum. Kangaroos, black
swans, pelicans, and long-legged wading birds roam the banks
and billabongs of this riverine border between Victoria and
New South Wales. The "mighty, muddy Murray" and its
tributaries drain a seventh of the continent; in the age
of steam, paddle wheelers plied this great highway, bringing
supplies to settlers, hauling crops, wool, and timber for markets
beyond the river mouth on the South Australia coast. Today,
steamboats fill with human cargo curious to taste the scenic
flavor of the lazy river. The antique* Adelaide *(above),
dating from 1866, chugs about in venerable retirement.*

Living symbols of Australia: Wattle trees bow under the weight of their golden blooms; settlers wove the limbs into their wattle-and-daub huts. Galah names a noisy parrot (above)—hence, also, a nitwit. The koala finds bed and board in gum trees.

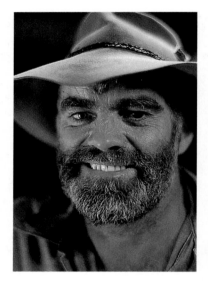

*Alpine stockmen ride
herd across the slopes of
Mount Eadley Stoney. Range
boss and son of the peak's
namesake, Graeme Stoney
(above) rides point in a
crusade to continue
traditional grazing here.
Stoney disputes claims that
the cattle endanger plant
life in the high country, a
rugged terrain encompassing
some of Victoria's most
breathtaking scenery.*

Morning brings the runners out at Surfers Paradise, where high rises press against

Queensland and New South Wales:
The Crowded Coast

the beach in one of the nation's fastest growing cities—part of Queensland's Gold Coast.

Australians aren't really irreligious, one of them has said— they worship beaches. Fortunately for the cult, about 80 percent of them live within 50 miles of a seacoast. Sydney's Bondi Beach is one of the historic shrines. Newer, but equally famous, is Surfers Paradise, on Queensland's Gold Coast about an hour's drive from Brisbane. I ran into an old-timer in Brissie who owned a house down there, bought years ago before outside investors raised the ante. "Today," he said, "the average Australian person, he probably couldn't afford it."

Thousands of those "average persons" come on holiday for a week or two. There're strong waves for the surfies, sand for the sunbakers, theme parks for the kiddies, glamour and glitz. Boom-and-bust growth inspired the tag "a sunny place for shady people," and some say it's an omen for Australia's future, a happy omen if you think concrete improves any landscape and all development is good.

Foreign investment has soared along with land values on the crowded eastern shores, especially in Queensland. Japanese interests have invested at least two billion *(Continued on page 168)*

Crystalline waters and colorful coral formations lure snorkelers to Australia's Great Barrier Reef, a complex of reefs, lagoons, and islands that stretches 1,200 miles along the Queensland coast. The reef, composed of 400 different types of corals, supports an incredibly rich ecosystem. Humpback whales and sea turtles breed here. Countless thousands of mollusks and other invertebrates and 1,500 fish species have adapted to life on the reef; they compete fiercely for food and space. A clown fish, covered by protective mucus, hides safely among a sea anemone's poisonous tentacles (below). Roomy catamarans carry increasing numbers of tourists to remote sections of the reef. Efforts to protect it led to establishment of the Great Barrier Reef Marine Park in 1975.

in Australian dollars, much of it in property on the Gold Coast. A campaign against foreign ownership sputtered a bit when the press identified its leader as a Kiwi; New Zealanders had bought more real estate than any other aliens. Queenslanders take pride in progress, but they are wary of outsiders, especially from southern states.

Queensland thinks big, plays big, is big. It's the northeast quadrant of the continent, and includes the Torres Strait Islands close to Papua New Guinea. At 667,000 square miles, it's more than twice the size of Texas and at least as proud. It boasts of assets like one of the world's largest deposits of bauxite and a ten-year population growth of 26.3 percent, almost double the national average. Below the border, the "southerners" call it the Deep North, with Dixie in mind.

In stereotype this Deep North is rural and parochial, racist and corrupt; also, a place of natural wonders and friendly folks, ideal for retirement. I found the positive side quite valid, the negative side changing. An independent official investigation was exposing some truly gaudy scandals in government, and I heard hopeful bits of news concerning the unhappy saga of black Queenslanders. Today they number about 61,000 including a few thousand Torres Strait Islanders living on the mainland. "Queensland has suddenly woken to the idea that Aboriginal culture is a gold mine," said one official; "it's an attraction for visitors." An ironic thought.

After British settlement began in 1824, with hardcase felons sent from Sydney, imported diseases and frontier warfare claimed ten or twenty thousand Aboriginal lives in Queensland. "Atrocity after atrocity over the years," one black leader said tersely. Henry Reynolds, a sandy-haired historian at the James Cook University, has given Australia a new knowledge of those conflicts. Until the 1850s, he told me, the spear could match the smoothbore musket. "The whites' crucial advantage was the horse, for speed and mobility. If some explorer in 1688 had left horses to run wild, I think the Aborigines would have adapted their culture to them as your Plains Indians did. The story might so easily have been different."

Instead, the settlers established a pastoral empire in the Queensland outback, and hoof-and-horn days live on around places like Longreach. This is the flat brown land, with horizons of sunburned grass and clouds like—naturally—fleece. Even the shearing sheds near Longreach were housing visitors when Queen Elizabeth II opened the Stockman's Hall of Fame during her bicentennial tour. As the U.S. had a Wild West, Australia had a Wild East as well, and the Hall collects relics of that era. The structure itself turns "tin-and-timber" makeshift into art. Its corrugated metal roofing curves in three graceful arcs, a silver-white blare in the sun. In midwinter, I enjoyed shirt-sleeve days and brisk nights here, and a motel cook told me that "Longreach mornings are always wonderful—crisp, clean—it makes you want to go out and kiss the earth."

Not on summer days. The heat around Cloncurry has buckled railroad steel, and at Mount Isa a crowbar laid flat on the ground gets too hot to be picked up. The mine at the Isa ranks as the free world's largest for silver and lead, one of the ten largest anywhere for copper and zinc. The tunnels once utilized one of Australia's amazing creations, an ultrasensitive strainmeter that can measure the minutest deformation of the earth.

Its inventor, Dr. Michael I. Gladwin, demonstrated the device in his physics lab at the University of Queensland. As in a seismograph, a pen squiggled on recording paper whenever he squeezed a sample of the copper ore being monitored. "It can easily measure shape changes as small as one-tenth of the diameter of one atom," he explained. His strainmeters are now monitoring some fault lines in California for minute changes that may precede earthquakes. "With this sensitivity, most solid objects seem alive. You can easily observe the deformation of the solid earth due to rain or wind on the surface."

"Queensland has the cream of Australia's natural history," says naturalist Vincent Serventy, and the Great Barrier Reef is the biggest of wonders. South of Cape York, screening the coast for 1,200 miles, it's a maze of more than 2,500 reefs, protected since 1975 as a marine park nearly as big as Montana. To see it all would take years. I sampled it. I started at the park's marine aquarium in Townsville, the ideal place to inspect sharks jaw to jaw. I watched sea anemones feeding, moving their tentacles in a graceful swaying hula, and admired a pair of little fish with turquoise-and-pink hulls and golden sterns. "You think you've seen the prettiest," said a plump matron beside me, "and then another comes by." That's it, in a seashell.

Nothing conveys the grandeur of the reef like an aerial view. Early one Sunday I joined a couple of parkies—marine park staff—on an air patrol from Cairns. We droned up into golden light, eastward over green isles and sandy cays and coral labyrinths that span the horizon. Deep channels ran a vibrant ultramarine; shallows ranged from pale blue to brown-gold; other reaches glowed in the subtle greens of weathered copper. Upsun the breeze raised tiny gold-foil crinkles over the slow advance of ocean swell. We watched in vain for dugong, the endangered sea mammal still common here. Near a sand islet called Beaver Cay, we looked for manta rays—and found one: a huge dark fish with pectoral fins like batwings ten feet long, flapping its uncanny slow-motion way through a lazy current.

A spot called Low Isles, mangrove habitat near Port Douglas, gives low-tide views of fauna from the intertidal zone—"a very, very harsh environment," explained the biologist guide on a beach walk. In the shallows, we saw soft corals that resembled spaghetti, or dishmops of thick yellow yarn. A few dead patches of hard coral had been smothered by mud carried down the Daintree River. Tough as reef creatures are, they're ill-prepared for pollution.

Gazing at the coast north of Port Douglas, from a speeding catamaran, I was thrilled to see nothing man-made. Forested highlands looked as pristine as Captain Cook saw them when he edged warily northward among the reefs in 1770. Squinting into sun dazzle, I understood how these uncharted waters had menaced his small *Endeavour* and why he named a headland Cape Tribulation. Perhaps, I thought, I got here just in time. One spire, one high rise, one anything would have broken that illusion of time transcended.

Tides measure the hours on the remote reefs. The run to Agincourt Reef crosses shallows where the Aborigines hunted 18,000 years ago, when sea levels were lower and the land was dry. This reef lies near the edge of the continental shelf. Even on a calm day, combers striking a coral rampart hurled their white spray high. The catamaran moored at an underwater observatory. A semisubmersible ferried a German party around the site. A dive master took the scuba mob to a trail of their own, and a small school of blue-finned snorkelers joined larger schools of fish in silky winter water, just cool enough. As the tour biologist said, "It's an animal garden, an animal landscape, an animal community with plants tucked inside."

One coral resembles a blue carnation; "cabbage-leaf coral" evokes a yellowed vegetable. Coral contours blur when the polyps protrude, feeding, fuzzing the hard surfaces with hungry tufts. In a marvelous synchrony many corals spawn en masse about 20 minutes after dark on the fourth or fifth night after the full moon in late spring. "The world's greatest sex orgy," a park executive calls it. The reefs are as full of riddles as of beauty. On a patch of white sand, little golden fish flit past electric-blue staghorn coral. Fingerlings glint blue-green like opal chips come alive. A massive Maori wrasse explains its common name; if fish played rugby, this two-foot-long bruiser would be an all-star forward. You think you've seen the funniest, the oddest, the prettiest, and then another comes by.

Reef meets Queensland's rain forest near the mouth of the Daintree River. During my visit officials in Canberra and state counterparts in Brisbane were wrangling over these forests. Canberra was seeking World Heritage status for a designated tract. Brisbane was opposed, denouncing what its leader called "bullyboy tactics." Shortly after, the status was granted, but Brisbane fought on in the courts.

A young southerner, biologist Jan Gorrie, guided me around in this disputed terrain. We visited an area in Daintree National Park where 1,100 species of trees compete for sunlight and nutrients. We clambered among vines and over buttress roots in a green dimness. "People often say, 'I thought it would be more jungly than this,'" Jan remarked. "There isn't enough light for dense undergrowth." These are plant communities with animals hidden inside. "The birds are small and ill-colored," she went on, "the flowers are small and dull, and 75 percent of the fruits are poisonous. Big bright flowers and birds are new, modern species. This is a relic of the old forest that covered the continent once."

North of the Daintree, in a tract reserved for science, we saw specimens of *Selaginella*, plants allied to the ancient club mosses and standing all of several inches high. "There were forests of them, 30 feet tall, 350 million years ago—before dinosaur times." Near a clear little stream, Jan picked up a drab green object, hard-shelled but cracked, the size of a tennis ball. "This is nicknamed 'idiot fruit.' It's the seed of *Idiospermum*. It's a hallucinogen, and *very* poisonous. It's one of the most primitive flowering plants in the world—the best example left of what the first flowering species were like." I held it briefly, trying to imagine what an unwary dinosaur's hallucinations might have been.

Jubilant delirium swept Canberra during my visit. The Canberra Raiders had reached the rugby league final, and Australia's capital reminded me of Washington when the Redskins reach the Super Bowl. As it happened, the Raiders lost, but Canberrans agreed that their city had found its soul at last.

Many observers have denied that it has one. Often it does seem to carry its heart in a briefcase, leaving one hand free to shoo bush flies in summer. After dark, I've been told, it's the most beautiful cemetery in Oz. As capital of a nation of knockers, it gets a year-round bashing. "It's always good business," a geographer told me in Queensland, "for state politicians to challenge the Commonwealth— 'our poor old beleaguered state against Big Nasty in Canberra.'" Aussie sentiments on politics range from polite skepticism to profane cynicism. The new Parliament House must be the only capitol designed to let citizens walk over the heads of the lawmakers. It nestles into the slopes of Capital Hill, with a walkway over the roof.

Parliament itself mixes British and American elements. As in London, the party with a majority in the lower chamber forms a government, led by a prime minister. If the government loses its majority, it must resign. But as in Washington, this chamber is called the House of Representatives; and the upper house, the Senate, is the stronghold of the states. A governor-general, normally apart from the political fray, represents the sovereign.

Radicals a century ago wanted a republic. In recent opinion polls, 30 to 40 percent concurred. Will they get one? I suspect the best prophecy is Dave Lindner's shirt-sleeves verdict from Kakadu National Park. "Naah," he drawled, "Australians are too lazy to think it out. Anyway, what difference does it make? If we wanted to get rid of the royals, they wouldn't resist. If they did resist"—a grin spread over his suntanned face—"it might be worth having a go."

Most compelling of Canberra's monuments is the Australian War Memorial, stoic as a fortress in pale masonry, visited by a million people a year. Its exhibits explain the feats of the Anzacs for those too young to remember, and there's a *(Continued on page 176)*

Pride on parade: Beribboned veterans march on Anzac Day in Cairns, as do

comrades across the land and in New Zealand, to honor men and women fallen in war.

*Another face of Australia: A family prepares for church
on Sue Island in the Torres Strait, where more than a hundred
islands dot the waters between Queensland and New Guinea.
Of Melanesian origins, the islanders have evolved a culture
of their own. Unlike Australia's Aborigines, the Torres Strait
people have remained on their ancestral lands, growing
crops and harvesting food from the sea. Boatmen beach their
craft after diving for giant clams. Long-standing disputes
over land and fishing rights, along with other grievances,
have fueled talk of independence.*

re-creation of a Vietnam setting, jungle and trail—so uncannily faithful, I heard, that one survivor of combat there can't force himself to enter it. In its cloister are the names of the war dead, listed without distinction of rank, honored for equality of sacrifice.

Such lists in New Zealand show Maori as well as European names. No Aboriginal names caught my eye in Canberra. I later learned that Aborigines were indeed included, but under the European names they used. Since they are not identifiable, Aboriginal servicemen have been left out of the national myth, said Maj. Bob Hall. He noted that more than 300 Aborigines served in World War I, more than 3,000 in World War II. Today, said the major, a historian and career soldier, army units in the north learn bushcraft from Aboriginal instructors.

Eric Willmot, director of the department of education in the Australian Capital Territory, has written a novel re-creating the story of Pemulwuy, the Rainbow Warrior, who emerged in the 1790s as the first leader of armed resistance to British settlement. "I heard it as a kid," he told me, "and found it in a book on early bushrangers." Until he was 20, Eric worked as a drover in the outback; today he's one of the few Aborigines honored in the Stockman's Hall of Fame, where I saw a photograph of him. Discussing his novel, Eric said his hero, Pemulwuy, was "a very clever guerrilla fighter who kept up his war until his death." The Rainbow Warrior used to camp, he said, on Bennelong Point, where the Sydney Opera House now stands, overlooking the city's matchless harbor.

The harbor gleams silver when the sun comes out of the Tasman Sea. It sparkles through the day as ships and small craft swirl white wakes into the blue. It flares sheet-gold at sunset and reflects the city's lights into darkness. It fills scores of coves and inlets, rippling between narrow headlands: bright water and green lawns, water and dark bush, water and cityscapes. "I cannot paint its loveliness," mourned England's great novelist Anthony Trollope in 1873. Any visitor, he said, would think of staying to look at the harbor "as long as he can look at anything." Or she. For years I've dreamed of a house with a harbor view, but waterfront prices have spiraled to seven or eight figures. Sydney, according to playwright David Williamson, is the Emerald City of Oz.

Sydney or the bush! It's a catchphrase. Go for broke, win or lose the lot. Sydney's flashy, raunchy, tough, posh. It's the fast track, the rat scramble. It's where the inner skyline rises ever more jagged; where VIPs enjoy five-star luxury at waterside and waifs from the little country towns drift into trouble near King's Cross. Rock bands deafen one pub after another: the Flying Emus, Redgum, Vegimite Reggae. In the faded working-class setting of Redfern, a group called Black Women's Action raises funds to support two students at

Harvard, U.S.A., while immigrants learn Aussie ways in the outer suburbs. Sydneysiders number about 3.5 million, three-fifths of the population of New South Wales and one-fifth of Australia's. Their red-roofed houses crowd a conurbation covering 1,600 square miles.

To the west, 60-odd miles from shore, the Emerald City is approaching the Blue Mountains. As Mark Twain saw them in 1895: "towering and majestic masses of blue—a softly luminous blue, a smoldering blue, as if vaguely lit by fires within." In fact that blue haze comes from eucalyptus leaves, an aerosol of oil. These sandstone scarps and pinnacles are a spur of the Great Dividing Range, between the dry interior and the coast.

Stubborn toffee-colored sandstone juts into the Tasman here and there, dividing one beach from another. In 1,200 miles of coastline, New South Wales boasts beaches rated as good, excellent, and magnificent. At some, sunbakers perfect their tans without benefit of even minimal bathing costume; at others, the trendies show off whatever fashion favors. In teenage circles, as two young women from the States assured me, the old Down Under male chauvinism lives on. "It's like the worst of Europe," said one. "It's so blatant, so innocent it's *almost* charming," said the other. Although the man's world mindset is changing in professional and business circles, it has deep roots here. Often, notes Robert Hughes, female convicts were "the prisoners of prisoners."

Britain's Australia began on a harbor beach where Circular Quay stands today. Here the ferries and cruise boats churn past the Sydney Opera House, gleaming on Bennelong Point. On January 26, 1788, Capt. Arthur Phillip, R.N., came ashore from H.M.S. *Supply* to raise the flag. He had brought the 11 small ships of the First Fleet 15,000 miles in 252 days. He had 6 civilians and 250 royal marines to guard some 700 surviving convicts. These included 71 highwaymen, and 31 muggers guilty of robbery by violence. Also a woman of 83 (given seven years for perjury) and a boy of 9 (seven years for stealing clothes and a pistol). Seven-year terms also avenged the theft of one live and one dead hen (total value fourpence), or 12 cucumber plants, or one packet of snuff.

I've boarded a ferry, or lingered over fine oysters at a waterside restaurant, or strolled amid jasmine at the Royal Botanic Gardens where those first felons struggled to start a farm, and I've tried to imagine that original summer. I've often wondered if the colonists' curses included George Washington, aptly called the stepfather of New South Wales.

Between 1717 and '76, Britain had sent about 40,000 convicts to its colonies in America, where free settlers hired their labor. Glumly making peace with the United States in 1783, George III wanted to send out more of the felons who were overcrowding his jails. The Americans did not oblige him. British officials decided to use the land that James Cook had claimed for the crown in 1770. They turned it into the world's largest prison. They didn't bother to make treaties with the natives, as was done in America and New Zealand. In Mark Twain's considered opinion, the Britain of the convict era was "a nation to whom the term 'civilized' could not in any large way be applied." Yet he found remarkable achievement here. Australian history, he concluded, was itself "the chiefest novelty" of the place. "It does not read like history, but like the most beautiful lies. And all of a fresh new sort, no moldy old stale ones. . . . but they are all true, they all happened."

Freshness still pervades both Sydney and the bush that urbanites can easily enjoy. North of the city, where parklands frame Broken Bay, weathered rock outcrops, thin-leafed gums, and feathery casuarinas suggest what Sydney's sunny waterways were like before the strangers came. And, as a friend pointed out on a trip to the Hunter Valley, it's only about two hours from the Opera House before a highway runs "as close to virgin scrub as you'd find."

In this coastal bush, the visiting poet-novelist D. H. Lawrence saw "invisible beauty." But that's strongest, I think, in a different landscape, the mallee scrub of the dry southeastern plains. Mallee grows in drab, spindly clumps, storing nutrients in massive woody roots that keep it alive through drought and fire. I saw it first on a drab, overcast day, and thought *how beautiful*, and then wondered why I thought any such thing. It's the beauty of survival against odds, the quintessence of the country as a living homeland.

Going into 1988, Australia was planning her official "celebration of a nation." Quite a few in other states were saying, "It's really a New South Wales show." As my geography adviser in Queensland had said, "It's very hard to get Australians to celebrate anything political." Eric Willmot had said, "It's very hard for us to believe in anything." A forest manager had this to say of the British: "Australians really don't like the Poms—Eureka Stockade, the whole scene—and here we are supposed to celebrate what they did." Some citizens had told me they would prefer to honor the centenary of federation, in 2001.

Would that date see New Zealand as a member state at last? Both nations had already decided upon closer economic relations. A Kiwi newspaper raised the old question of a formal union. One reader praised the idea as "the most sensible thing that could happen." "Have you gone nuts?" fumed another. A third wanted no part of "a country founded on criminals." Under the pen name Status Quo, one suggested that Australia improve her treatment of the Aborigines; then she might be admitted to New Zealand "as the West Island."

To many Aborigines, 1988 was a whitefellas' show. John Moriarty in Adelaide had told me, smiling, "Let them celebrate 200 years. We have 200 times 200 years." Traditional artists had devised a special exhibit for urban galleries; it featured the funeral pole that

David Malangi had painted in Arnhem Land, set up with 199 others as if each year equaled a death. Communities across the nation collected money and cars and "freedom buses" to meet in Sydney and march in protest on Australia Day, January 26.

Meanwhile, nine small vessels were battling financial woes to re-enact the voyage of the First Fleet, and the world's Tall Ships were on course for Sydney. From the Netherlands came the 75-foot schooner *Abel Tasman*, whose namesake mariner had added New Zealand and much of Australia's coasts to European maps in the 1640s. The tallest of the lot—like Japan's *Nippon Maru* or the U.S. Coast Guard's *Eagle* or Poland's *Dar Mlodziezy*—eased warily under the Harbour Bridge at low tide, to moorings just west of Sydney Cove. Here, at Darling Harbour, the state was converting dilapidated waterfront into gardens and plazas and a new museum of maritime history. Crowds turned out in thousands, and over the holiday weekend they reached coral-reef density.

I found a calmer center of interest at Mrs. Macquarie's Chair. Here, on a sandstone ledge, a governor's lady used to rest and gaze over the harbor while her husband, Lachlan Macquarie, struggled to change a prison camp into a free community. Those who paid their debt to society, he thought, should enjoy the rights of citizens as self-respecting equals. Against the odds, many individuals succeeded in doing just that. Here, for the nation's festival, Aboriginal leaders had set up a "tent embassy" under the red-black-and-yellow banner of land rights.

A burly man with strong-boned features posed for scores of cameras in a cape with "LAND IS LIFE" emblazoned on the back. This was Graham Silva, an urban Aborigine. Patiently, he discussed his cause with questioners, some friendly, some not.

A thin blond with hair younger than her face posed a question with undertones of scorn: What had his people done with the country when they had it? Graham put prehistory into a sentence: "We kept it, and it kept us." "Humpf." She left. A barefoot, wiry old battler said he had made it through the Great Depression without ever going on the dole, and he insisted that anyone who tried hard could do as well now; then he surprised me by holding out a gnarled hand to Graham's, saying, "Good luck, mate."

The grand observance of Australia Day followed a Monday when quite a few took an unofficial holiday. Public transport conveyed two million people to the shores and waters of Sydney Harbour. Families with strollers and eskies, insulated coolers that sustain the good life in Oz, were streaming along to good vantage points even at dawn. After the sun cleared the skyscrapers, the foreshores glittered like mica as sunlight flashed from camera lenses and sunglasses and cold tinnies. Dignitaries gathered in a courtyard behind the Opera House. First Fleet descendants in 1788 costume took front-row seats. A guard of honor appeared in historic uniforms, including the garb of the 42nd Somersetshires who had attacked the Eureka Stockade.

Small craft brought guests of high public rank, with the Prince and Princess of Wales as first royal guests of the year.

As premier of New South Wales, the Premier State, Barrie Unsworth had the honor of saying "Welcome, Australia! Welcome, the world!" He spoke of the nation's "worst possible beginning" and its expanding future. Prime Minister Robert Hawke, in his "G'day mate" accent, declared that commitment to Australia is the one true bond in a nation of diversity. "In Australia," he said, "there is no hierarchy of descent; there must be no privilege of origin."

The Heir to the Throne spoke next. In the purest Queen's English, Prince Charles recalled his teenage education in Oz, "when I had the Pommy bits bashed off me." He praised the discoveries of Captain Cook, and he didn't gloss over the misery of the colony "where inconvenient people could be transported and forgotten." The best part of the story, he said, "is that they made their prison into a new home," where in time freedom became "a reality for everybody." It would be hard to answer Aboriginal protests, he conceded, "beyond suggesting that a country free enough to examine its own conscience is a land worth living in, a nation to be envied."

Out on the blue ripples, where the little First Fleet vessels came in to their anchorage, anything that would float was swerving and bobbing around. The state sent the old harbor ferry *Supply* into the thick of it with TV crews and print journalists to capture the glory of the day. About 4,000 boats cruised around, or rested in a cheerful gridlock, from the luxurious yacht of tycoon Alan Bond to a raft paddled by two boys who were giving their dog a good view. One runabout displayed a placard of sardonic realism: "27th—HANGOVER OF A NATION."

Police boats scurried like sheepdogs to keep a channel clear for the Tall Ships' parade of sail. On the bridge of the research vessel H.M.A.S. *Cook*, Prince Charles in a digger hat took the salutes. An unmistakable figure in her emerald silk, Lady Diana waved greetings. Ecuador's bark *Bae Guayas* glided past with musicians playing a sultry "Waltzing Matilda." Now and then I heard cheers ring out: "*Hoch! Hoch! Hoch!*" from West Germany's *Gorch Fock*, "*Jai! Jai! Jai!*" from India's *Varuna*.

"Di! Di! Di!" yelled suntanned blokes in small boats, brandishing beers for Her Royal Highness. Security patrols shunted them away, but one boat slipped through to let two topless beauties trade grins with the Prince. Sydney just wouldn't be Sydney without that raffish streak. It's the style of the larrikin, the street-smart young Aussie with a lot of bravado, ready to spill tomato sauce on any stuffed shirt, and it has flourished here since Sydney town was young.

"This is the best day of my life!" declared an Aussie journalist (male) when *Supply* finally turned shoreward. A colleague (female) added cool approval of the day's events: "Very Sydney." Everything had gone smoothly, happily. Some twenty or thirty thousand Aborigines and Torres Strait Islanders had gathered; their march went peacefully, with somber dignity, as its leaders had promised. One of them told me later, happily, "It was brilliant—a brilliant day!"

That was Bob Weatherall from Toomelah, a big man with a long beard, a stockman's hat, and a big laugh. He can relate tragic stories from the past, heartening stories from his work with young people in Brisbane. He summed up Australia Day, 1988, with eloquence. "We were all gathered together. You know the slogan? 'One Mob, One Voice, One Land.' We saw how the culture of 40,000 years has survived. We will not die, we will not go away. The wheels are turning—things are changing—we'll see how the game's to be played."

Red afterglow lingered in the west and red warnings flickered from the channel buoys when *Supply* went out for the night's finale of fireworks. Music drifted on the breeze from the Opera House plaza; on the North Shore, the Ferris wheel at Luna Park traced its small festive circle of light. *Supply* edged into Sydney Cove, where her namesake had moored precisely two centuries earlier for a first night's vigil in the rustling shadows of the bush.

Suddenly, crimson rockets soared over the sails of the Opera House and the water gleamed like smoldering coals. White sparkles of flashbulbs twinkled along the shores. From three points on the harbor the projectiles whirred upward, tracing paths of brightness as if miraculous serpents had flashed across the dark. Deep-toned rumbles of sound thrummed on the air. Sunbursts of brilliance opened overhead and showered color on the mirror rippling below: flares of gold, spheres of light as if dandelion puffs had turned to meteors; crimson points spreading into starfish patterns; sprays of violet and gold and blue. Silver-white laceworks dazzled the eye like glints from tin-roof metal, and their sheen danced in the water.

There's a Maori blessing that hints at such magic: ". . . may the sea glisten like the greenstone, and may the golden rays of summer dance across your pathway." At last, a diadem of enormous tapers blazed from the arch of the Harbour Bridge and a glorious cascade of light poured down from the span, a golden waterfall of radiance, and then the last cheers died away and it was time for home. □

FOLLOWING PAGES: Sandstone escarpments rim the Grose River Valley in Blue Mountains National Park, due west of Sydney. The mountains, actually a plateau etched by two rivers, barred expansion until 1813, when explorers followed a ridgeline across them.

ROBIN SMITH

GRENVILLE TURNER / WILDLIGHT;   ROBIN SMITH (RIGHT)

Brawny stockmen observe the Aussie ritual of smoke-o,
a break (theoretically a short one); and a lone tramper
observes another, boiling the billy—heating a can of
water for tea in the bush. The setting suggests the
world-famous ballad "Waltzing Matilda," cherished as
an unofficial national anthem. Matilda refers to a
bedroll, or swag; and the song's swagman—an itinerant
looking for work, perhaps, or simply a rover—ranks as
a hero for very Australian reasons. In the lyrics by A. B.
("Banjo") Paterson, he's jolly, however down on his
luck. He takes a stray jumbuck (sheep) for food. The
squatter who owns it would run thousands of sheep on
thousands of acres and probably acquired his land
by bending the law; but he's keen to prosecute the poor
tramp. Drowning himself to die a free man, the
swagman defies unjust power—and his ghost,
singing at his last campsite, still haunts the bush.

Together wherever they go, a grey kangaroo and her joey share a meal at a nature reserve near Canberra. Marsupials—the name comes from the pouch in which most females carry their young—inhabited the land millions of years ago, when it became an island continent. Isolated in Australia, marsupials thrived; in other lands placental mammals replaced them. The only egg-laying mammals in the world, the echidna and the platypus (right), live in Australia. The platypus lays its eggs in streamside burrows. The emu (opposite) cannot fly but may sprint at 30 mph. The male emu incubates the eggs and raises the chicks. Second-tallest bird in the world, the emu ranks behind the ostrich.

Previewing Canberra's new Parliament House prior to its dedication in 1988, visitors queue up to enter the Great Veranda. Centered in the pool behind them, a mosaic (right) of Aboriginal design represents the island continent and the first Australians. Steel emu and kangaroo support the shield of state above the entrance. From the new veranda the vista engages past glories, the old Parliament House and, beyond it, the Australian War Memorial.

GRENVILLE TURNER / WILDLIGHT

© MICHAEL JENSEN / AUSCAPE;   PHILIP QUIRK / WILDLIGHT (RIGHT)

*All work and one plays at
two of Sydney's 24 beaches.
A surfer rules the waves
at Bronte, and a rescue
team plows through them
in a drill at Bondi. Heroic
figures, members of surf
lifesaving clubs represent
the paragon of manhood
to many Australians.
Lifesavers, disciplined and
conservative, clash with the
free spirits of surfing;
but Aussies of all stripes
prize their beaches.*

Two strong traditions meet peacefully in Sydney on Bicentennial Australia Day: January 26, 1988. Some 20,000 Aborigines from all over the nation march in protest. A descendant of the First Fleet wears period dress for ceremonies at the Opera House, where Diana, Princess of Wales, appears in emerald silk. The Prince sports a tie in green and gold, the colors of Australia's national teams. On the 13th, a bearded elder had watched a team of famous cricketers play the National Aboriginal Cricket Team, which later toured England, as an unofficial native team did in 1868: an Aussie first.

OLIVER STREWE / WILDLIGHT (ALSO ABOVE)   CAROLYN JOHNS / WILDLIGHT (ALSO ABOVE)

FOLLOWING PAGES: Two hundred years to the night after the British stepped ashore at Sydney Cove, fireworks flare over its waters. The peaked roofs of the Opera House and the span of the Harbour Bridge stand out in radiance.

CAROLYN JOHNS / WILDLIGHT

Glossary

Surprising lands, surprising words, surprising sounds. New Zealand's language, enriched with Maori expressions, resembles Britain's English, though with distinctive pronunciations. Australian vernacular is rich and expressive, sometimes coarse; one form, dubbed Strine, employs rhyming slang and—to alien ears—mystifying compressions. The sampler below includes a number of words appearing elsewhere in the book, none coarse, not all vernacular.

avago: *have a go*

barracking: *cheering for your team*

battler: *one who fights the odds, hangs in*

billy: *tin can for boiling water*

bitumen: *asphalt paving; hence, highway*

bloke: *guy (good bloke: great guy)*

bush: *rural area, backcountry*

bush tucker: *wild edibles*

crook: *sick, broken-down, useless*

drongo: *dimwit*

fair dinkum: *honest*

fair go: *fair chance, level playing field*

garbo: *garbageman in Strine*

greenie: *conservation activist*

hoon: *fool, idiot*

larrikin: *street rowdy, rascal*

mate: *buddy, colleague*

mob: *any group; not a gang*

ocker: *Archie Bunker Down Under*

outback: *backcountry*

Pom, Pommy: *Britisher, usually English*

sealed road: *blacktop road*

she'll be right: *it'll work out; no worries*

she's sweet: *she'll be right*

shout: *a round of drinks*

smoke-o: *tea break, smoke break*

whinge: *complain, whine, gripe*

wowser: *officious moralist, killjoy*

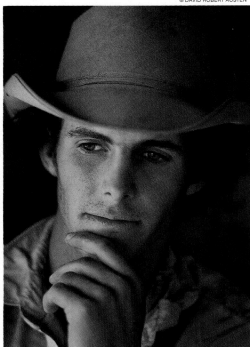

© DAVID ROBERT AUSTEN

A young stockman pauses to reflect in the lonely outback of northern Queensland.

A NOTE ON THE AUTHOR

Mary Ann Harrell, a member of the Society's staff since 1958, has played a key editorial role in some three-fourths of the 94 Special Publications that preceded this one. She plans to edit the one-hundredth, *Pathways to Discovery.* She has also been a principal author of public service books on the Supreme Court and the White House. She was born in Durham, N.C., and earned degrees at Wellesley and at the University of North Carolina.

ACKNOWLEDGMENTS

The Special Publications Division is grateful to embassy and other officials of New Zealand and Australia for their cooperation. We appreciate the courtesies extended at marae in New Zealand and by Aboriginal and Torres Strait islander groups in Australia. We thank also the individuals and organizations named herein, and those cited here:

New Zealand: Clarence Beeby, Michael Benjamin, Elisabeth B. Booz, Phyllida Bunkle, Elizabeth Caffin, Kevin P. Clements, Mr. and Mrs. Frank Corner, Denis Dutton, Lauris Edmond, Mr. and Mrs. Joe Everitt, Roger Green, Antonia Macedo, Sidney Moko Mead, Jan Morrison, Elizabeth Orr, Jock Phillips, Peter Rankin, Wallace Rosenberg.

Australia: Len Beadell, Peter Bellwood, Steve Carapetis, Carrick Chambers, Mr. and Mrs. J.R.J. Clark, Manning Clark, Jeff Clarke, Claire Darling, Peter Edwards, Toby Gangele, Nene Gare, Mr. and Mrs. John Graham, Allan Griffiths, Peter Hiscock, Rhys Jones, Erica Kyle, Fred Longbottom, Isabel McBryde, Dr. and Mrs. Charles Miller, Margaret Reynolds, Dr. and Mrs. Paul L. Robertson, Derek Roff, Mrs. Vincent Serventy, Sheryl Vickery. For help in the states, the Australian Overseas Information Service staff; and in the Northern Territory, Hilary Tims and Denham Jones.

Library of Congress ⊂⊞ Data

Harrell, Mary Ann.
Surprising lands down under.
  1. Australia—Description and travel—1981-
2. New Zealand—Description and travel—1981-
I. National Geographic Society (U.S.). Special Publications Division. II. Title.
DU105.2.H37 1989   994   89-14499
ISBN 0-87044-714-9 (regular edition)
ISBN 0-87044-719-X (library edition)

Index

Boldface indicates illustrations; *italic* refers to picture captions.

ADDITIONAL READING

The reader may wish to consult the National Geographic cumulative index for pertinent references, and to watch for American editions of notable works from Down Under. Of the many books consulted, those mentioned in the text and the following may be of special interest.

For New Zealand: Russell J. Beck, *New Zealand Jade;* James Belich, *The New Zealand Wars;* Betty Brownlie, *The Secrets of Natural New Zealand;* David Lewis, *The Maori, Heirs of Tane;* Claudia Orange, *The Treaty of Waitangi;* Margaret Orbell, *The Natural World of the Maori;* Anne Salmond, *Hui;* Maurice Shadbolt, *Voices of Gallipoli;* Keith Sinclair, *A Destiny Apart* and *A History of New Zealand.*

For Australia: Jeremy Beckett, *Torres Strait Islanders;* Ronald M. and Catherine H. Berndt, *The First Australians* and *End of an Era;* Linda Christmas, *The Ribbon and the Ragged Square;* Manning Clark, *A Short History of Australia;* Peter Conrad, *Down Home;* Frank Crowley, *et al.,* eds., *Australians: A Historical Library* (ten vols.); Michael Dugan and Josef Szwarc, *There Goes the Neighborhood!;* Josephine Flood, *Archaeology of the Dreamtime;* Stephen R. Graubard, ed., *Australia: The Daedalus Symposium (Daedalus,* winter 1985); Bill Hornadge, *The Australian Slanguage;* Henry Reynolds, *Frontier, The Other Side of the Frontier,* and *The Law of the Land;* Derek Roff, *Ayers Rock & The Olgas;* Jane Ross, *The Myth of the Digger;* Ronald Strahan, ed., *Complete Book of Australian Mammals;* Peter Sutton, ed., *Dreamings: The Art of Aboriginal Australia.*

Composition by the Typographic section of National Geographic Production Services, Pre-Press Division. Printed and bound by R. R. Donnelley & Sons, Willard, Ohio. Color separations by Graphic Art Service, Inc., Nashville, Tenn.; Lanman Progressive Co., Washington, D.C.; Lincoln Graphics, Inc., Cherry Hill, N.J.; and NEC, Inc., Nashville, Tenn. Dust jacket printed by Federated Lithographers-Printers, Inc., Providence, R.I.

TITLE IX
LEVELS THE
PLAYING FIELD

BY RACHEL AXON

WOMEN IN SPORTS

SportsZone

An Imprint of Abdo Publishing
abdopublishing.com

abdopublishing.com

Published by Abdo Publishing, a division of ABDO, PO Box 398166, Minneapolis, Minnesota 55439. Copyright © 2018 by Abdo Consulting Group, Inc. International copyrights reserved in all countries. No part of this book may be reproduced in any form without written permission from the publisher. SportsZone™ is a trademark and logo of Abdo Publishing.

Printed in the United States of America, North Mankato, Minnesota
042017
092017

Cover Photo: AP Images
Interior Photos: AP Images, 1, 21; Rebecca Blackwell/AP Images, 4–5; Henry Burroughs/AP Images, 7; Joe Marquette/AP Images, 8; Michael Spomer/Cal Sport Media/AP Images, 10–11; Gary Blakeley/Shutterstock Images, 13; AJ Mast/AP Images, 14; Paul Connell/The Boston Globe/Getty Images, 16–17; Press Association/AP Images, 19; Tony Dejak/AP Images, 22; Alex Tsarik/Shutterstock Images, 25; Aspen Photo/Shutterstock Images, 26; Jessica Hill/AP Images, 28, 44; Anthony S. Bush/Topeka Capital-Journal/AP Images, 30; Phelan M. Ebenhack/AP Images, 31; Ray Stubblebine/AP Images, 32–33; LM Otero/AP Images, 34; Douglas Graham/CQ-Roll Call Group/Getty Images, 36; Martin Meissner/AP Images, 38–39; Markus Schreiber/AP Images, 40; Kristy Wigglesworth/AP Images, 41; Paul Sancya/AP Images, 42

Editor: Patrick Donnelly
Series Designer: Laura Polzin
Content Consultant: Rita Liberti, PhD, Professor of Kinesiology, California State University, East Bay

Publisher's Cataloging-in-Publication Data

Names: Axon, Rachel, author.
Title: Title IX levels the playing field / by Rachel Axon.
Description: Minneapolis, MN : Abdo Publishing, 2018. | Series: Women in sports | Includes bibliographical references and index.
Identifiers: LCCN 2017930236| ISBN 9781532111570 (lib. bdg.) | ISBN 9781680789423 (ebook)
Subjects: LCSH: Athletes--Juvenile literature. | Women athletes--Juvenile literature. | Sports for women--Juvenile literature. | Sex discrimination in sports--Juvenile literature.
Classification: DDC 796--dc23
LC record available at http://lccn.loc.gov/2017930236

TABLE OF
CONTENTS

CREATION OF TITLE IX

The text of the landmark law is just 37 words. Neither "sports" nor "athletics" are mentioned. Yet no law has done so much to shift the landscape of sports for girls and women.

"No person in the United States shall, on the basis of sex, be excluded from participation in, be denied the benefits of, or be subjected to discrimination under any education program or activity receiving Federal financial assistance."

Passed as part of the Education Amendments of 1972, Title IX has done more than merely increase opportunities for women in sports. It has changed the culture to such an extent that the United States now boasts a wealth of female athletes, sports journalists, coaches, and officials. For pro athletes such as Serena Williams and Ronda Rousey, and for Olympians such as Simone Biles and

Gymnast Simone Biles and other female athletes have benefitted from the passage of an important law in 1972.

Katie Ledecky, opportunity in sports wouldn't have been possible without Title IX.

Before the passage of Title IX, women faced extreme obstacles just to be allowed to compete. There were outstanding female athletes before 1972, of course. But the belief that women were not interested in sports was widespread. Some even believed that competing could be physically harmful to women.

That began to change in the 1970s, thanks in part to Edith Green, a member of the US House of Representatives from Oregon. Green introduced a bill that would work toward equity between men and women in higher education. In hearings she described the discrimination women faced on a routine basis. She argued that action was necessary for equality to be achieved.

Green's arguments were influential. Indiana Senator Birch Bayh introduced Title IX as an amendment to an

Congresswoman Edith Green walks the corridors of the Rayburn House Office Building in 1967.

US Representative Patsy Mink of Hawaii played an important role in defending Title IX in Congress.

education bill. The bill passed, and President Richard Nixon signed it into law.

Amazingly, it received little attention at the time, as more contentious issues such as school desegregation also were addressed in the amendments. But its impact would be vast and profound. Title IX bans federally funded educational programs from discriminating on the basis

PATSY MINK

While Edith Green argued for equality in the early 1970s, Representative Patsy Mink of Hawaii defended the law after Green left Congress in 1974. After Mink's death in 2002, the law was renamed to the Patsy T. Mink Equal Opportunity in Education Act in her honor.

of gender. It applies to a music program or school play as much as it does to athletics.

In 1972 only 1 in 27 high school girls participated in athletics in the United States. That amounted to 294,015 girls. By 2015–16 that total had increased tenfold to more than 3.3 million girls competing at the high school level.

But Title IX did more than just mandate equality in opportunities. It required parity in all areas—the facilities used by male and female athletes, the equipment available to them, and the salaries of their coaches, among others.

To be sure, many more battles lie ahead for women in sports. Equality can remain elusive at times. But the passage of Title IX changed the paths and lives of every American girl and woman, from 1972 to today.

THE FIGHT CONTINUES

Though Title IX passed in 1972, the fight for equality in education was far from over. In many ways, it was just beginning as legislators and lawsuits sought to alter and curb the law. In 1974 Texas Senator John Tower introduced an amendment to exempt revenue-producing sports such as football from the law's requirements. That would have allowed schools to once again pour money into their football programs without spending an equal amount on women's athletics. The amendment was rejected.

The US Department of Health, Education, and Welfare issued its regulations in 1975 that schools had three years to comply with Title IX. By 1978 that had not happened. Opponents of the law continued to challenge it. They gained a victory in 1984 when the US Supreme Court ruled in *Grove City College v. Bell*. It said only programs that received federal funds had to comply with Title IX. For instance, a private school such as Grove City College had to comply because it provided federal scholarships. But it did not have to adhere to Title IX in

Opponents of Title IX have argued that college football should not count when determining equity between men's and women's opportunities.

its athletics program because it did not receive federal funding for sports.

Congress reversed the effects of that decision in 1988, passing the Civil Rights Restoration Act by overriding a veto from President Ronald Reagan. The act fully implemented the law and required schools to comply no matter what kind of federal assistance they received.

At that point Title IX had existed for nearly 16 years, but many schools still were not compliant with the law. The battle continued. In 1992 the Supreme Court ruled in *Franklin v. Gwinnett County Public Schools* that plaintiffs

YALE ROWING

In 1976 the women's rowing team at Yale University made a powerful protest against inequity. In their case, the men's team had showers but the women's team could not shower after practice. The athletes had to ride a bus back to campus while cold and wet.

The team protested to a school administrator while naked, writing Title IX on their backs. Captain Chris Ernst read a statement that said, in part, "These are the bodies Yale is exploiting." The women got their showers.

Some Title IX lawsuits have made it all the way to the US Supreme Court.

could receive damages when schools tried to avoid complying with Title IX. Two years later, Congress passed the Equity in Athletics Disclosure Act. It requires colleges

and universities to record and report to the Department of Education information on athletic participation, staffing, revenues, and expenses for their intercollegiate athletics programs. Finally, in 1996 the Department of Education's Office for Civil Rights issued a clarification on the effective implementation of the law.

Nearly 25 years after Title IX passed, it had survived many challenges. It finally had some teeth to enforce it. Schools had regulations to follow and reporting requirements to the government that would help enforce them.

The National Collegiate Athletic Association (NCAA) challenged the legality of Title IX in 1976. But it ended up publishing a landmark gender equity study and creating a task force to study gender equity issues in 1992.

Certainly more challenges did and likely will continue to come. But as the law neared its 25th anniversary, it had gained the tools needed to ensure equality for girls and women in sports.

Once an opponent of Title IX, the NCAA has come to support the massive expansion of athletic opportunities.

IMPACT ON WOMEN'S SPORTS

From today's perspective, it's almost impossible to envision the sports landscape for women before Title IX. The Women's National Basketball Association (WNBA) was born in 1997. The US soccer team won the Women's World Cup in 1999. Tennis star Serena Williams is one of the most dominant athletes of her generation. To modern observers, the pre-Title IX views and attitudes about women in sports can seem almost foreign.

Yet examples of the struggles that female athletes faced are numerous. For example, it took until 1967 for Kathrine Switzer to become the first woman to run the Boston Marathon with a numbered entry. The historic race allowed only men to

A race official, *partially hidden*, tries to drag Kathrine Switzer off the course at the 1967 Boston Marathon.

participate for its first 70 years. Switzer got around that by signing up as "K. V. Switzer." A race official tried to drag Switzer from the course, but her boyfriend shoved him away and Switzer finished the race.

Other facts seem equally unfathomable. In 1971, the year before Title IX was passed, only 28 schools in the country had girls' soccer teams. Their rosters comprised just 700 players. In the 1970s, high school girls played six-on-six basketball in parts of the country. Three players were guards who stayed in the backcourt, while three forwards stayed in the frontcourt. As with many sports at that time, girls and women were considered too frail to play a full-court game. The widespread acceptance we have for girls and women in sports today simply did not exist before Title IX was passed.

"Ladylike" sports such as golf or tennis were deemed acceptable. But many believed women were not interested in strenuous or contact sports and were too weak to compete in them.

Jump forward to nearly a half century after Title IX was passed: attitudes have changed significantly. Soccer is now one of the most popular sports for girls, trailing only

Tennis was one of the few sports deemed acceptable for women to play in prior eras.

basketball, volleyball, and track and field in the number of high school participants. More than 3.3 million girls competed in high school sports in 2015–16. That's an increase of more than 1,000 percent from 1971–72.

OPTIONS ABOUND

Before Title IX, it wasn't only a lack of opportunities that girls and women faced. It was a lack of options in what sports were acceptable to play. Golf, tennis, and swimming were more common. The year the law passed, high school girls didn't compete in ice hockey, rugby, lacrosse, or wrestling. Thousands of girls now participate in those sports.

Opportunities have increased at the college level for women as well. Swimmer Donna de Varona won two gold medals in the 1964 Summer Olympics but ended her career at age 17 because she could not get a college scholarship. Tennis legend Billie Jean King first won at Wimbledon in 1966, but she never received a college scholarship either. Athletic scholarships for women simply didn't exist then. In 1974 Ann Meyers became the first woman to receive a four-year athletic scholarship when she signed to play basketball at the University of California, Los Angeles (UCLA).

In 1971–72, approximately 30,000 women competed in college athletics. In 2015–16, the NCAA reported 211,886 women participating in college sports. That growth of

Donna de Varona holds one of her gold medals from the 1964 Summer Olympics.

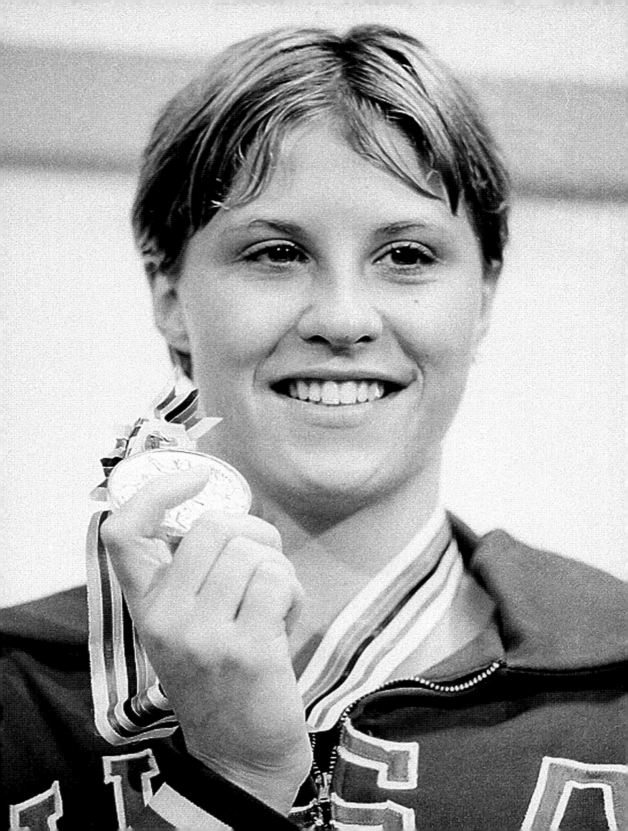

opportunity extended to women's coaching, as well, although that rate has declined in recent years. In 1972 90 percent of women's college teams were coached by women. According to a 2014 study, that number had fallen to

> No coach embodied the success of Title IX more than Pat Summitt. She became the University of Tennessee women's basketball coach in 1974 when she was just 22 years old. She retired 38 years and eight national championships later, and her 1,098 wins were a Division I record for men or women.

43.4 percent. One possible reason for that decline is that male coaches may now view women's sports as legitimate, not a lesser version of men's sports.

Without question more progress can be made. But it's no exaggeration to say nothing has shifted the landscape of sports for girls and women more than Title IX. It can be measured in opportunities and scholarships. And it can be felt in the acceptance women have experienced in pursuing their athletic goals. The notion of "playing like a girl" has gone from an insult to a point of pride. That's thanks in large part to Title IX.

Pat Summitt, *right*, gives instructions to star player Candace Parker in 2007.

4

THE NUTS AND BOLTS OF TITLE IX

The premise of Title IX is pretty simple—schools receiving federal funds cannot discriminate on the basis of gender. If boys and men can play, so can girls and women.

But how does the government ensure schools are complying with Title IX?

The Department of Education's Office for Civil Rights (OCR) has created a three-prong test that allows schools to demonstrate that they are following the law. Each school must meet one of the following criteria:

1. **Proportionality**—Schools must compare the ratio of male and female athletes to the ratio of male and female students enrolled. The schools need to ensure those ratios are close. Say, for instance, a school's student body is 55 percent female. In order to comply with Title IX, that school would need to make 55 percent of its athletic opportunities available for girls or women.

Title IX was designed to create equity in opportunities for men and women.

Women's college soccer has seen incredible growth thanks in part to Title IX.

2. **History and continuing practice**—Schools must show that they have a history of adding opportunities for the underrepresented sex and continue to do so.

3. **Accommodating interest**—Schools must show they are effectively accommodating the interests of the underrepresented sex.

It's important to note that schools themselves choose which of these prongs they use to comply. In the decades since Title IX passed, the proportion of undergraduate college enrollment for women has increased from around 41 percent in 1970 to more than 50 percent today. Many more opportunities for participation in sports exist for boys and men than for girls and women at the high school and collegiate levels. That makes proportionality a difficult avenue by which to achieve compliance.

Many Division I schools face problems in balancing out the 85 scholarships they can offer in football. That has prompted the rapid growth of some sports, such as rowing and soccer, for women. From 1981 to 2016, 60 Division I schools added women's rowing and 306 added women's soccer teams.

Title IX also calls for equity in other areas. Scholarships must be allocated proportionate to the size of the men's and women's programs.

Men's and women's teams must be treated equitably in regards to the quality of their uniforms, facilities, schedules, and coaching, among many other things. Contrary to some beliefs, the law does not require

LACK OF INTEREST OR OPPORTUNITY?

Since Title IX was passed, schools have argued that women are less interested in sports than men are. But in 1996 in *Cohen v. Brown University*, a federal appeals court rejected that argument from the school and ruled that Brown discriminated against female athletes. As has been shown throughout Title IX's history, women are interested in sports and embrace them when given the opportunity.

exact equity. It recognizes that football equipment, for example, costs much more than the equipment required for swimming.

But it does require that schools ensure the experiences are comparable for their men's and women's teams. That means sometimes allowing girls to play on boys' teams. Because girls largely remain the underrepresented sex in athletics, the law requires they be allowed to try out for a boys' team if there is no girls' team in that sport. For instance, a female cross country runner could compete on a boys' team if there is not a girls' team at her school.

Title IX dictates that women's athletic facilities—from arenas to locker rooms to weight rooms—must be equitable.

But it doesn't work the other way. Boys have more opportunities than girls, so allowing them to compete on a girls' team would take away opportunity from the underrepresented sex.

Wrestling is one sport in which girls have had to compete on boys' teams.

Track and field is another sport that has provided many opportunities for college female athletes.

It's up to the OCR to enforce the law. It can investigate complaints or decide on its own to review a school's compliance with Title IX. Schools that don't comply risk losing their federal funding, which can amount to millions of dollars. While OCR has never revoked that money from a school, it serves as a powerful motivator. Schools out of compliance usually work with OCR to make changes to their athletic programs.

CHAMPIONS OF TITLE IX

S ince Title IX was passed, the law has been defended and championed by many women and men. But a few noteworthy women stand out as steadfast advocates for the law as they pushed over decades for enforcement and acceptance of Title IX.

Billie Jean King was a remarkable tennis champion, winning 67 singles titles and 39 major championships in her career. Despite that, she is perhaps best known for the "Battle of the Sexes," a 1973 match against Bobby Riggs, a 55-year-old former Wimbledon champion. Riggs said he could beat the top women's players because they were far inferior to men.

King easily won the match. She acknowledged the pressure she felt that night: "I thought it would set us back 50 years if I didn't win that match," she said.

King founded the Women's Sports Foundation (WSF) in 1974, a year after the "Battle of the Sexes." Since retiring

Billie Jean King was a champion on and off the tennis court.

Donna Lopiano speaks after receiving the NCAA President's Gerald R. Ford Award in 2013.

WOMEN'S WORLD CUP

The US victory in the 1999 Women's World Cup became iconic after Brandi Chastain ripped off her jersey following her winning penalty kick. But that team was already iconic because of its relationship with Title IX. Many of its players had been among the first women to receive college soccer scholarships. After Team USA's win in the 1991 Women's World Cup received little attention, the final in 1999 at the Rose Bowl in Pasadena, California, was played in front of the largest crowd to watch a women's sporting event at the time. The win sparked a further explosion of growth of the sport, even inspiring some of the girls who would eventually be part of the US team that won the 2015 Women's World Cup.

from tennis in 1983, she has continued to advocate for women in sports.

She got a lot of help from Donna Lopiano. As a young girl in the 1950s, Lopiano couldn't play Little League baseball because of a rule that barred girls from competing. She would go on to become a national champion softball player before starting a career as a coach and administrator.

Lopiano made a name for herself at the University of Texas, where she served 18 years as the Director of

US soccer star Julie Foudy, *right*, meets with US Representative Nancy Pelosi to discuss Title IX funding in 2003.

Intercollegiate Athletics for Women. Then she became the chief executive officer of the WSF. Lopiano testified before the US Congress three times regarding Title IX and gender equity in sport. And in 2013 Lopiano received the NCAA

President's Gerald R. Ford Award, which honors a person who has "provided significant leadership as an advocate for intercollegiate athletics on a continuous basis over the course of their career."

Following her own successful career, soccer star Julie Foudy used her voice in support of Title IX. She had benefited directly from the law, earning a scholarship to play at Stanford University. Foudy was a member of the US teams that won the Women's World Cup in 1991 and 1999 and Olympic gold medals 1996 and 2004.

Foudy and her teammates tried to make a professional soccer league work in the United States, but the Women's United Soccer Association (WUSA) never took off. Financial troubles brought the WUSA to a halt in 2003 after three seasons. Foudy then turned her attention to advocating for women's sports, with Title IX a particular focus. In 2004 she testified before Congress to defend the law and ensure its long-term viability.

TITLE IX'S LEGACY

For a view of how Title IX has changed sports for US girls and women, look to the 2016 Olympics in Rio de Janeiro, Brazil. For a second consecutive Summer Games, the Americans sent more women than men, as a record 292 women were part of the 555-member team.

That team included women who delivered remarkable performances. Gymnast Simone Biles used her high-flying tumbling to win five medals. Swimmer Katie Ledecky's dominance in the pool also yielded five medals. Boxer Claressa Shields won the first Olympic gold in women's boxing in 2012 and followed it with a win in 2016.

The US women dominated again at the 2016 Olympics in Rio de Janeiro.

Helen Maroulis celebrates after winning the gold medal in the women's 53-kg freestyle wrestling event at the 2016 Olympics.

That made her the first American to win back-to-back boxing golds.

Helen Maroulis won the USA's first wrestling gold for a woman. The US women's rowing eight won its 11th consecutive major title and third consecutive Olympic gold. And for the second Summer Olympics in a row, the US women brought home more medals than the men.

Almost none of that would have been possible without Title IX. Since the law passed, the explosive growth of opportunities has changed the game for girls and women in sports. But just as critically, the law has been responsible for a cultural shift in how women in sports are viewed. No longer are women considered disinterested or too frail to compete. And they've taken advantage of those opportunities. Where doors have been opened for them to participate, they have rushed through and embraced sports and all its benefits.

The number of girls and women playing has had a ripple effect. Certainly the Olympic teams benefit from collegiate sports serving as a developmental system. But it has also had an impact in areas such as sports journalism as well.

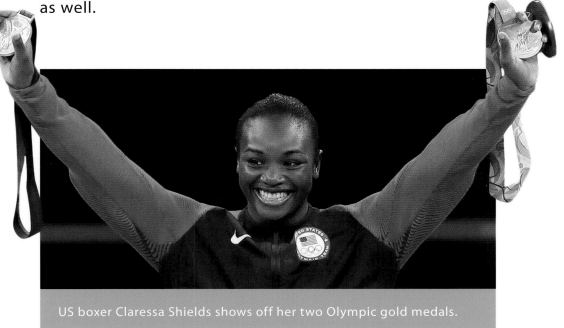

US boxer Claressa Shields shows off her two Olympic gold medals.

As advocates fought for Title IX in the decades after it passed, women in sports journalism fought for equity as well. While male reporters could go into locker rooms to interview athletes, female reporters were commonly barred from doing that into the 1980s.

February 3 has been named National Girls and Women in Sports Day. The day seeks to promote girls embracing physical activity.

Pioneering sports journalists such as Claire Smith, Lesley Visser, Melissa Ludtke, Robin Herman, Jane Gross, and Michele Himmelberg fought for that access. They helped women gain ground in the profession. While they make up a small portion of newsrooms, women have reached milestones since.

Doris Burke, Rachel Nichols, and Jessica Mendoza are among many female role models in sports broadcasting. If it's acceptable for girls and women to play sports, it's acceptable for women to cover sports.

Yet for all the progress Title IX has created, women in sports continue to face many challenges. Men still receive millions more in scholarship dollars. Colleges spend much

Rachel Nichols is a former newspaper reporter who made a successful transition to television.

Elena Delle Donne, *11*, and Lindsay Whalen, *4*, helped the US women's basketball team win its sixth straight Olympic gold medal in 2016.

more money on their men's programs. Coaches of men's teams make more on average than coaches of female teams in similar sports.

HOOP DREAMS

Basketball was the most popular sport among high school girls when Title IX passed. Today it is second only to track and field. Its growth in the high school and collegiate ranks led to the creation of the WNBA in 1997. Americans have dominated the Olympics ever since. In Rio the US women's basketball team won its 49th consecutive game and sixth consecutive gold medal.

The number of athletic opportunities for high school girls today still lags behind those available for boys in 1972. Men have more opportunity than women in college athletics, too. And although the number of opportunities for men has increased since 1972, Title IX is often falsely blamed for cuts to men's programs.

So the work of Title IX is not done. Equity is still many years away.

But the sports world that girls and women inhabit today is vastly improved since their mothers and grandmothers were denied the chance to play. They have Title IX to thank for much of that progress.

GLOSSARY

AMENDMENT
A change or addition to a bill.

ATHLETIC SCHOLARSHIP
Money provided to a student-athlete to pay for his or her education.

COMPLIANCE
Acting in a way that follows the rules or directions.

DISCRIMINATION
Making a distinction based on the group a person belongs to rather than on individual merit.

DIVISION I
The top level of competition in collegiate sports.

EQUITY
Fairness or impartiality.

FEDERAL FUNDING
Money received from the US government.

LANDMARK
Important, standing out among the rest.

PLAINTIFF
A person who brings legal action.

UNDERREPRESENTED SEX
The gender, typically girls and women, that has fewer opportunities in a program.

BOOKS

Hall, Brian. *Pioneers in Women's Sports*. Minneapolis, MN: Abdo Publishing, 2018.

Ignotofsky, Rachel. *Women in Sports: 50 Fearless Athletes Who Played to Win*. Berkeley, CA: Ten Speed Press, 2017.

Schiot, Molly. *Game Changers: The Unsung Heroines of Sports History*. New York: Simon & Schuster, 2016.

WEBSITES

To learn more about women in sports, visit **abdobooklinks.com**. These links are routinely monitored and updated to provide the most current information available.

PLACE TO VISIT

NCAA Hall of Champions
700 West Washington Street
Indianapolis, Indiana 46204
317-916-4255
ncaahallofchampions.org
The Hall of Champions is a museum and conference center built next to the NCAA offices. Interactive exhibits detail the exciting history of collegiate athletics and provide hands-on experiences through sports simulators and recreations of historic venues.

INDEX

ABOUT THE AUTHOR

Rachel Axon is a newspaper reporter originally from Western New York. She graduated from St. Bonaventure University in 2006. During her newspaper career, she has worked for the Wilmington (North Carolina) *StarNews*, the *Orlando Sentinel*, and *USA Today*. Axon has covered everything from high school sports to college football and the Olympics.